Descendants of Thomas Payne

Generation 1

1. **THOMAS**[1] **PAYNE** was born in 1660 in Rappahannock County, Virginia. He died in 1698 in Essex County, Virginia. He married (1) **MARY MONTAGUE**, daughter of Peter Montague and Mary Minor on 24 Oct 1682 in Middlesex County, Virginia. She was born about 1664 in Middlesex County, Virginia. She died before 17 Feb 1687 in Virginia. He married (2) **ELIZABETH ELLIOTT** about 1695. She was born in 1680.

   More About Mary Montague:
   b: 1664
   Burial: 17 Feb 1687

   Thomas Payne and Mary Montague had the following children:

   2. i. THOMAS[2] PAYNE was born in 1686 in Middlesex County, Virginia. He died on 19 Apr 1761 in Essex County, Virginia. He married (1) CATHERINE LYDFORD, daughter of Matthew Lydford and Lettice Weeks on 26 May 1715 in Middlesex County, Virginia. She was born in 1693 in Middlesex County, Virginia. She died in 1745 in Middlesex County, Virginia. He married (2) JANE BUSH in Virginia.

   ii. FRANCIS PAYNE was born in 1685 in Middlesex County, Virginia.

   iii. JOHN ELLIOTT PAYNE.

Generation 2

2. **THOMAS**[2] **PAYNE** (Thomas[1]) was born in 1686 in Middlesex County, Virginia. He died on 19 Apr 1761 in Essex County, Virginia. He married (1) **CATHERINE LYDFORD**, daughter of Matthew Lydford and Lettice Weeks on 26 May 1715 in Middlesex County, Virginia. She was born in 1693 in Middlesex County, Virginia. She died in 1745 in Middlesex County, Virginia. He married (2) **JANE BUSH** in Virginia.

   Notes for Thomas Payne: Will
   Dated February 16, 1758. Will
   Probated April 20, 1761.

   Thomas Payne and Catherine Lydford had the following children:

   3. i. REUBEN[3] PAYNE was born about 1732 in Middlesex County, Virginia. He died between 14 Sep 1819-08 Jan 1820 in Lincoln County, Kentucky. He married Agnes Wade, daughter of Joseph Wade in 1752 in Pittsylvania County, Virginia. She was born about 1730 in Virginia. She died before 14 Sep 1819 in Lincoln County, Kentucky.

   ii. THOMAS PAYNE was born on 19 Nov 1721 in Middlesex County, Virginia. He died in 1799.

   iii. JOHN PAYNE was born on 01 Dec 1722 in Middlesex County, Virginia. He died in 1780 in Pittsylvania County, Virginia. He married MARY (UNKNOWN). She died in 1767 in Halifax County, Virginia. He married ELIZABETH (UNKNOWN).

   iv. LETTICE PAYNE was born on 08 Aug 1716 in Middlesex County, Virginia.

   v. FRANCES PAYNE was born on 15 Mar 1719 in Middlesex County, Virginia.

   vi. CATHERINE PAYNE was born on 29 Jan 1725 in Middlesex County, Virginia.

    vii.   MARY PAYNE was born in 1729 in Essex County, Virginia.

    viii.   WILLIAM PAYNE was born in Middlesex County, Virginia. He died in 1818 in Pittsylvania County, Virginia. He married Sarah Nance, daughter of John Nance in Middlesex County, Virginia. She was born in Virginia. She died in Virginia.

    ix.   PHILLIMAN PAYNE was born in Middlesex County, Virginia.

Generation 3

3.   **REUBEN[3] PAYNE** (Thomas[2], Thomas[1]) was born about 1732 in Middlesex County, Virginia. He died between 14 Sep 1819-08 Jan 1820 in Lincoln County, Kentucky. He married Agnes Wade, daughter of Joseph Wade in 1752 in Pittsylvania County, Virginia. She was born about 1730 in Virginia. She died before 14 Sep 1819 in Lincoln County, Kentucky.

More About Reuben Payne: Military
Service: Revolutionary War

Notes for Reuben Payne:
Will dated September 14, 1819 and proven in Lincoln County, Kentucky January 8, 1820.

Reuben Payne and Agnes Wade had the following children:

    i.   MILLICENT[4] PAYNE was born in 1752 in Pittsylvania County, Virginia. She died in 1837. She married EDMUND J. FITZGERALD. He was born in 1745 in At Sea. He died in Pittsylvania County, Virginia.

    ii.   CATHERINE PAYNE was born about 1758 in Pittsylvania County, Virginia. She married William Parks on 24 Dec 1780 in Pittsylvania County, Virginia. He was born in 1758.

5.   iii. PHILEMON PAYNE was born on 28 Apr 1759 in Pittsylvania County, Virginia. He died in 1833 in Wayne County, Kentucky. He married Rachel Wilson, daughter of John Wilson and Elizabeth Hardin on 24 May 1787 in Pittsylvania County, Virginia. She was born in 1767 in Virginia. She died in 1828 in Wayne County, Kentucky.

6.   iv. LUCRETIA PAYNE was born in 1761 in Pittsylvania County, Virginia. She died in 1819 in Pittsylvania County, Virginia. She married John Pigg, son of William Pigg and Mary Fields on 28 Oct 1787 in Pittsylvania County, Virginia. He was born on 14 Apr 1769 in Pittsylvania County, Virginia. He died on 28 May 1811 in Clark County, Kentucky.

7.   v. EDMUND PAYNE was born in 1762 in Pittsylvania County, Virginia. He died in May 1825 in Barren County, Kentucky. He married Mary Hill, daughter of James Hill about 02 Jun 1795 in Barren County, Kentucky. She was born in 1770 in Virginia. She died in Barren County, Kentucky.

8.   vi. REUBEN PAYNE was born about 1763 in Pittsylvania County, Virginia. He died about 1821 in Lincoln County, Kentucky. He married (1) ELIZABETH PIGG, daughter of William Pigg and Mary Fields on 26 Aug 1790 in Lincoln County, Kentucky. She was born about 1778 in Albemarle, Virginia. She died on 02 Apr 1855 in Russell County, Kentucky. He married PARTHENA MITCHELL.

9.   vii. LABAN PAYNE was born about 1767 in Virginia. He died about 1846 in Kentucky. He

married Mary Edmondson Gray, daughter of James Gray and Lucy Webb on 28 Aug 1795 in Lincoln County, Kentucky. She was born on 14 Oct 1779 in Virginia. She died on 28 Oct 1858 in Grayville, White County, Illinois.

viii.   ELIZABETH PAYNE was born about 1769 in Pittsylvania County, Virginia. She married WILLIAM JONES.

ix.   MARY PAYNE was born about 1770 in Pittsylvania County, Virginia. She married (UNKNOWN) FOSTER.

Generation 4

4.   PHILEMON[4] PAYNE (Reuben[3], Thomas[2], Thomas[1]) was born on 28 Apr 1759 in Pittsylvania County, Virginia. He died in 1833 in Wayne County, Kentucky. He married Rachel Wilson, daughter of John Wilson and Elizabeth Hardin on 24 May 1787 in Pittsylvania County, Virginia. She was born in 1767 in Virginia. She died in 1828 in Wayne County, Kentucky.

Philemon Payne and Rachel Wilson had the following child:

i.   JOHN WILSON[5] PAYNE. He married AGNES PAYNE.

5.   LUCRETIA[4] PAYNE (Reuben[3], Thomas[2], Thomas[1]) was born in 1761 in Pittsylvania County, Virginia. She died in 1819 in Pittsylvania County, Virginia. She married John Pigg, son of William Pigg and Mary Fields on 28 Oct 1787 in Pittsylvania County, Virginia. He was born on 14 Apr 1769 in Pittsylvania County, Virginia. He died on 28 May 1811 in Clark County, Kentucky.

John Pigg and Lucretia Payne had the following children:

i.   FRANCES[5] PIGG.

ii.   AGNES PIGG. She married JOHN PARKS.

iii.   WILLIAM PIGG.

iv.   PATSY PIGG.

v.   REUBIN PIGG.

vi.   JOHN PIGG.

vii.   LABAN PIGG.

viii.   LUCRETIA PIGG was born before 1802 in Clark, Kentucky. She died on 13 Feb 1886. She married Samuel Cornett on 08 Aug 1823 in Clay County, Kentucky.

6.   EDMUND[4] PAYNE (Reuben[3], Thomas[2], Thomas[1]) was born in 1762 in Pittsylvania County, Virginia. He died in May 1825 in Barren County, Kentucky. He married Mary Hill, daughter of James Hill about 02 Jun 1795 in Barren County, Kentucky. She was born in 1770 in Virginia. She died in Barren County, Kentucky.

Notes for Edmund Payne:

Marriage Bond is dated June 2, 1795.

1825 WILL OF EDMUND PAYNE

In the name of God Amen, I Edmund Payne of the County of Barren and the state of Kentucky being low in
health and weak in body, but in my right mind for which I thank God, I do hereby make and ordain this my
last Will and Testament in manner and form following,

Viz. 1st, I desire that all the perishable property part of my estate be left on my plantation under the care of my wife Mary Payne and children. If any of my children should marry or chose to leave the premises after coming of age I wish my Executors hereafter named, to let them to have such necessaries as they judge can be made equal without distressing the family.
2ndly, If my wife Mary Payne should marry, I wish there to be a sale of all my estate , and her to have a child's part during her natural life and after her decease, to return back to my children to be equally divided among them, (Excepting?) any of my children should chose their share in land I would wish them to have the privilege if they will take. unreadable sentence??.
3rdly if my wife Mary Payne should die before my youngest children come of age, I wish there to be a sale, as aforesaid, and the money arising there from to be equally divided among my children, Reuben Payne, Elizabeth Payne, Catherine Payne, Agness Payne, Edmund Payne, Lettice Payne, Lucretia Payne, Nathan Payne, Vincent Payne, to be (enjoyed?) by them forever.
4thly if my wife Mary Payne should continue to live a widow until my youngest children come of age, I wish her to have one half of my plantation including the house, orchard, and six acres of woodland beginning at the upper side of the apple orchard, and running towards the meadow, and also my Negro man Bob, and one fourth part of the perishable property during her natural life and then to return to my children aforementioned and to be equally divided among them, and the balance of my estate sold when my youngest children comes of age. If any of my children should have more than another before the sale I wish it then be made equal. I wish my four youngest children: Lettice, Lucretia, Nathan, Vincent to have schooling as much as is convenient, I would wish that the money I have in hand to be made use of in the best manner it can for the support of the family Also what is owing to me(?).
And lastly I do hereby constitute and appoint my friend William Parks and Reuben Payne executors of this my last Will and Testament, hereby revoking all other former Wills by me heretofore made, In witness whereof I have hereunto set my hand and seal --
(Edmund Payne)
       seal

Attest Frederick Tanner
David Lyen, William Lyen
Barren County to wit, May County Court 1825
The foregoing writing purporting to be the Last Will and Testament of Edmund Payne deceased, was produced in Court and proven by the oaths of David Lyen and William Lyen, subscribing witnesses whereupon the said writing was ordered to be recorded as the true Last Will and Testament of the said Edmund Payne Dec'd, which hath been duly entered of record accordingly.
      attest:signed _____?

Edmund Payne and Mary Hill had the following children:

    i.   REUBEN[5] PAYNE was born about 1796. He died in 1844 in Barren County, Kentucky.

        Notes for Reuben Payne:
        Will dated December 19th 1843.
        Will proven January term of Barren County Court 1844. (Kentucky)

        Dec 19th 1843
        In the name of God Amen I Reuben Payne of the County of Barren and state of

Kentucky being sick and weak in body but of sound mind and disposing memory, for which I thank God, and calling to mind the uncertainty of human life and being desirous to dispose of all such worldly estate as it hath please God to bless me with I give and bequeath this same in manner as following that is to say

-1st I desire that all the perishable part of my estate be immediately sold after my death and any of the moneys arising there from all my just debts and funeral expenses be paid

-2ndly After the payment of my debts and funeral expenses I give sister Catherine Payne who is intermarried with William Kidwell one dollar

- 3rdly I give to my sister Elizabeth Payne who is intermarried with William Pedego one dollar

- 4thly I give and bequeath to Agness Payne married to Melton Witty and Edmond Payne and Letty Payne and Lucretia Payne and Nathan Payne and Vincent Payne the balance of my personal and real estate to be equally divided between my last named brothers & sisters which I give to them their heirs executors administrators and assigns forever

- And lastly I do hereby constitute and appoint my friends Edmond Payne and Vince Payne executors of my last will and testament hereby revoking all other former wills or testaments by me heretofore made. In witness whereof I have hereunto let my hand and affixed my seal.

attest
Reuben Payne
(seal) Wade Volugat
Joel Sartain

Barren County Crt January Term 1844
The foregoing writing purporting to be the last will of Reuben Payne decd was produced in court and proven in the form of law by the oath of Wade Veluzah and Joel Sartain subscribing witnesses thereto whereas the same was ordered to be recorded as the true last will of said Reuben Payne decd.

----

9.   ii. CATHERINE PAYNE was born about 1798 in Kentucky. She died after 26 Jul 1870. She married WILLIAM KIDWELL. He was born about 1794 in Virginia. He died in Jul 1859 in Monroe County, Kentucky.

      iii. ELIZABETH PAYNE was born in 1800 in Kentucky. She died after 30 Aug 1850. She married (1) WILLIAM PEDIGO on 25 Nov 1841 in Glasgow, Barren County, Kentucky. She married (2) RALPH PETTY on 21 Oct 1847 in Barren County, Kentucky. He was born about 1768 in Virginia. He died after 30 Aug 1850.

10.   iv. AGNES PAYNE was born on 10 Mar 1803. She died on 30 Sep 1848 in Barren County, Kentucky. She married Milton Witty, son of Ezekiel Witty and Jane Cummins on 22 Jan 1824 in Barren County, Kentucky. He was born on 11 Dec 1803 in North Carolina. He died on 15 Apr 1864 in Metcalfe County, Kentucky.

11.   v. EDMUND PAYNE was born in 1805 in Kentucky. He died before 04 Sep 1850. He married Elvira Witty, daughter of Ezekiel Witty and Jane Cummins on 06 Jul 1825 in Barren County, Kentucky. She was born about 1811 in North Carolina. She died after 28 Jun 1880.

      vi. LETTICE PAYNE was born in 1813 in Kentucky. She died after 19 Jul 1860.

More About Lettice Payne:
Living In: 1850 Living with her brother, Vincent, and his family in Barren County, Kentucky.
Living In: 1860 Living with her brother, Vincent, and his family in Beat 4, Hunt County, Texas.

Notes for Lettice Payne:
Possibly Deaf

12.   vii. LUCRETIA PAYNE was born about 1815 in Kentucky. She died on 17 Sep 1857 in Barren County, Kentucky. She married Phillip A. Shive on 17 Dec 1846 in Barren County, Kentucky. He was born about 1823 in Kentucky. He died between 12 Aug 1870-05 Jun 1880.

13.   viii. NATHAN PAYNE was born on 09 Mar 1816 in Barren County, Kentucky. He died on 21 Oct 1880 in Lone Oak, Texas. He married Mary Elizabeth Glass, daughter of Benjamin Glass and Susanna Franklin on 15 Jul 1841 in Barren County, Kentucky. She was born on 08 Feb 1822 in Barren County, Kentucky. She died on 01 Dec 1880 in Lone Oak, Texas.

14.   ix. VINCENT S. PAYNE was born in 1819 in Barren County, Kentucky. He died in 1865 in Hunt County, Texas. He married Mildred Glass, daughter of Benjamin Glass and Susanna Franklin on 13 Jan 1842 in Glasgow, Barren County, Kentucky. She was born on 02 Apr 1827 in Barren County, Kentucky. She died on 28 Oct 1883 in Hunt County, Texas.

7.   **REUBEN**[4] **PAYNE** (Reuben[3], Thomas[2], Thomas[1]) was born about 1763 in Pittsylvania County, Virginia. He died about 1821 in Lincoln County, Kentucky. He married (1) **ELIZABETH PIGG**, daughter of William Pigg and Mary Fields on 26 Aug 1790 in Lincoln County, Kentucky. She was born about 1778 in Albemarle, Virginia. She died on 02 Apr 1855 in Russell County, Kentucky. He married **PARTHENA MITCHELL**.

More About Elizabeth Pigg:
Living In: 1850 Russell County, Kentucky

Reuben Payne and Elizabeth Pigg had the following child:
     i.   AGNES[5] PAYNE. She married JOHN WILSON PAYNE.

8.   **LABAN**[4] **PAYNE** (Reuben[3], Thomas[2], Thomas[1]) was born about 1767 in Virginia. He died about 1846 in Kentucky. He married Mary Edmondson Gray, daughter of James Gray and Lucy Webb on 28 Aug 1795 in Lincoln County, Kentucky. She was born on 14 Oct 1779 in Virginia. She died on 28 Oct 1858 in Grayville, White County, Illinois.

Notes for Laban Payne:
Lived in White County, Illinois from about 1826 until 1833.

More About Mary Edmondson Gray:
Living In: 1850 With her son, William, in Hancock County, Kentucky

Notes for Mary Edmondson Gray:
Died in Grayville, White County, Illinois while on a visit from Kentucky.

Laban Payne and Mary Edmondson Gray had the following children:

i. W ILLIAM L .[5] P AYNE was born on 16 Apr 1818 in Kentucky. He died on 03 Mar 1907 in Illinois. He married CATHERINE BALDAUF. She was born on 04 Dec 1830 in Germany. She died on 08 Jun 1916 in Grayville, White County, Illinois.

More About William L. Payne:
Burial: Oak Grove Cemetery, Grayville, Edwards County, Illinois
Living In: 1900 Gray Township, White County, Illinois
Occupation: 1850 in Hancock County, Kentucky; Saddler
Military Service: Bet. 17 Nov 1862-15 Apr 1863; Captain of Company H, 12th Kentucky Cavalry, U.S.A.

Notes for William L. Payne:
Born in kentucky. Lived in White County, Illinois from about 1826 until 1833 when he returned with his parents to Kentucky. Moved back to White County, Illinois in 1863.

Grayville, Illinois is in White and Edwards counties.

Resigned his commision as captain of company H, 12th Kentucky Cavalry on April 7, 1863 because of a tumor on his right shoulder. Resignation was accepted on April 15, 1863.

ii.   ALEXANDER PAYNE was born in Kentucky.

iii.   MARY J. M. PAYNE was born in Kentucky.

Generation 5

9.   CATHERINE[5] PAYNE (Edmund[4], Reuben[3], Thomas[2], Thomas[1]) was born about 1798 in Kentucky. She died after 26 Jul 1870. She married WILLIAM KIDWELL. He was born about 1794 in Virginia. He died in Jul 1859 in Monroe County, Kentucky.

More About Catherine Payne:
Living In: 1870 Living with her nephew, Joseph Reuben Witty, and his family in Sartain, Metcalfe County, Kentucky.

More About William Kidwell:
Cause Of Death: Fever is given on Federal Census Mortality Schedule
Occupation: 1850 in Monroe County, Kentucky; Farmer

William Kidwell and Catherine Payne had the following children:

i.   ANNIE[6] KIDWELL was born about 1823 in Kentucky.

ii.   ISHAM KIDWELL was born on 30 Jan 1829 in Kentucky. He died on 22 Dec 1914 in Monroe County, Kentucky.

More About Isham Kidwell:
Burial: 23 Dec 1914 in Oak Hill Cemetery, Tompkinsville, Monroe County, Kentucky
Occupation: Farmer

iii.　CATHERINE KIDWELL was born about 1833 in Kentucky.

10.　AGNES[5] PAYNE (Edmund[4], Reuben[3], Thomas[2], Thomas[1]) was born on 10 Mar 1803. She died on 30 Sep 1848 in Barren County, Kentucky. She married Milton Witty, son of Ezekiel Witty and Jane Cummins on 22 Jan 1824 in Barren County, Kentucky. He was born on 11 Dec 1803 in North Carolina. He died on 15 Apr 1864 in Metcalfe County, Kentucky.

More About Milton Witty:
Occupation: 1850 in Division 2, Barren County, Kentucky; Farmer
Occupation: 1860 in Metcalfe County, Kentucky; Farmer

Milton Witty and Agnes Payne had the following children:

i.　JAMES[6] WITTY was born about 1827 in Kentucky.

More About James Witty:
Living In: 1850 Living with his father and step mother in Division 2, Barren County, Kentucky.
Occupation: 1850 in Division 2, Barren County, Kentucky; Farmer

ii.　EZEKIEL WITTY was born on 02 Nov 1829 in Barren County, Kentucky. He died on 14 Mar 1915 in Metcalfe County, Kentucky. He married MARTHA E. PACE. She was born on 18 Nov 1834. She died on 10 Nov 1916 in Summer Shade, Metcalfe County, Kentucky.

More About Ezekiel Witty:
Burial: Summer Shade Cemetery, Summer Shade, Metcalfe County, Kentucky
Living In: 1850 Living with his father and step mother in Division 2, Barren County, Kentucky.

iii.　JOSEPH REUBEN WITTY was born on 19 Nov 1831 in Kentucky. He died on 16 Jul 1898. He married MARY F. HUFFMAN. She was born on 06 Aug 1842. She died on 10 Apr 1919.

More About Joseph Reuben Witty:
Burial: Summer Shade Cemetery, Summer Shade, Metcalfe County, Kentucky
Living In: 1850 Living with his father and step mother in Division 2, Barren County, Kentucky.
Living In: 1860 Living with his father and step mother in Metcalfe County, Kentucky.
Occupation: 1870 in Sartain, Metcalfe County, Kentucky; Retail Dry Goods Merchant

iv.　MILTON WITTY was born about 1834 in Kentucky.

More About Milton Witty:
Living In: 1850 Living with his father and step mother in Division 2, Barren County, Kentucky.

11.　EDMUND[5] PAYNE (Edmund[4], Reuben[3], Thomas[2], Thomas[1]) was born in 1805 in Kentucky. He died before 04 Sep 1850. He married Elvira Witty, daughter of Ezekiel Witty and Jane Cummins on 06 Jul 1825 in Barren County, Kentucky. She was born about 1811 in North Carolina. She died after 28 Jun 1880.

More About Elvira Witty:
Living In: 1850 Division 2, Barren County, Kentucky
Living In: 1860 Metcalfe County, Kentucky
Living In: 1870 Sartain, Metcalfe County, Kentucky
Living In: 1880 Summer Shade, Metcalfe County, Kentucky

Notes for Elvira Witty:
Living two doors away from Milton Witty in 1850.

Edmund Payne and Elvira Witty had the following children:

    i.   MARY[6] PAYNE was born about 1829 in Kentucky.

    ii.   AMANDA PAYNE was born about 1831 in Kentucky.

    iii.   ELIZABETH C. PAYNE was born about 1833 in Barren County, Kentucky. She married William Martin on 16 Sep 1856 in Barren County, Kentucky. He was born about 1835 in Barren County, Kentucky.

    iv.   CATHERINE PAYNE was born about 1835 in Kentucky.

    v.   ALBINA PAYNE was born in Mar 1837 in Kentucky. She married JOHN WILSON. He was born in May 1829 in Indiana.

    vi.   ELVIRA F. PAYNE was born about 1843 in Kentucky.

    vii.   REUBEN PAYNE was born about 1845 in Kentucky.

    viii.   MARTHA E. PAYNE was born about 1848 in Kentucky.

    ix.   MELDON W. PAYNE was born about Dec 1849 in Kentucky.

    x.   SALLY S. PAYNE was born about Dec 1849 in Kentucky.

12.   **LUCRETIA[5] PAYNE** (Edmund[4], Reuben[3], Thomas[2], Thomas[1]) was born about 1815 in Kentucky. She died on 17 Sep 1857 in Barren County, Kentucky. She married Phillip A. Shive on 17 Dec 1846 in Barren County, Kentucky. He was born about 1823 in Kentucky. He died between 12 Aug 1870-05 Jun 1880.

More About Phillip A. Shive:
Occupation: 1850 in Division 2, Barren County, Kentucky;
Farmer
Occupation: 1860 in Metcalfe County, Kentucky; Farmer
Occupation: 1870 in Lincoln, Hendricks County, Indiana; Farmer

Phillip A. Shive and Lucretia Payne had the following children:

    i.   NANCY CATHARINE[6] SHIVE was born about 1848 in Kentucky.

        More About Nancy Catharine Shive:
        Living In: 1860 Living with her father and step mother in Metcalfe County, Kentucky.
        Living In: 1870 Living with her father and step mother in Lincoln, Hendricks County, Indiana.

    ii.   HENRY C. SHIVE was born about Jun 1850 in Kentucky.

        More About Henry C. Shive:
        Living In: 1860 Living with his father and step mother in Metcalfe County, Kentucky.

13.   NATHAN[5] PAYNE (Edmund[4], Reuben[3], Thomas[2], Thomas[1]) was born on 09 Mar 1816 in Barren County, Kentucky. He died on 21 Oct 1880 in Lone Oak, Texas. He married Mary Elizabeth Glass, daughter of Benjamin Glass and Susanna Franklin on 15 Jul 1841 in Barren County, Kentucky. She was born on 08 Feb 1822 in Barren County, Kentucky. She died on 01 Dec 1880 in Lone Oak, Texas.

More About Nathan Payne:
Burial: Hall Cemetery, Lone Oak, Hunt County, Texas
Occupation: 1850 in Division 2, Barren County, Kentucky; Farmer
Occupation: 1860 in Precinct 9, Hunt County, Texas; Farmer
Occupation: 1870 in Precinct 4, Hunt County, Texas; Farmer
Occupation: 1880 in Precinct 4, Hunt County, Texas; Farmer
Military Service: Bet. 12 Sep-31 Dec 1863 in Greenville, Hunt County, Texas; Enlisted in Company E, 2nd Cavalry, Texas State Troops, C.S.A.
Property: 1860 in Hunt County, Texas; 25 Acres Improved and 631 Acres Unimproved

Notes for Nathan Payne:
Moved to Hunt County, Texas between 1852 and 1855, probably 1853.

More About Mary Elizabeth Glass:
Burial: Hall Cemetery, Lone Oak, Hunt County, Texas

More About Nathan Payne and Mary Elizabeth Glass:
Marriage Fact: Married by Reverend Thomas J. Malone

Nathan Payne and Mary Elizabeth Glass had the following children:

15.   i.   WILLIAM[6] PAYNE was born on 06 Nov 1842 in Barren County, Kentucky. He died on 2 Nov 1909 in Denton, Texas. He married Mary Francis Weatherly, daughter of Augustus Graham Weatherly and Elizabeth Jane Harrison on 06 Dec 1865 in Hunt County, Texas. She was born on 19 Sep 1848 in Paulding County, Georgia. She died on 10 Apr 1915 in Denton, Texas.

    iii.   BENJAMIN PAYNE was born on 04 May 1844 in Barren County, Kentucky. He married LILLY (UKNOWN).

        More About Benjamin Payne:
        Military Service: Civil War for C.S.A.

        Notes for Benjamin Payne:
        Died in the Civil War

16.   iii.   EDMUND PAYNE was born on 29 Jun 1846 in Barren County, Kentucky. He died on 22 May 1919. He married Mary Virginia Harrison, daughter of John Harrison and Rhoda Gordon on 27 Mar 1867 in Hunt County, Texas. She was born on 05 Jan

1850 in Georgia. She died on 27 Apr 1929.

17. iv. ANDREW ALEXANDER PAYNE was born on 09 May 1848 in Barren County, Kentucky. He died on 07 Oct 1920 in Lone Oak, Hunt County, Texas. He married Carrie Weatherly, daughter of Isaac C. Weatherly and Rachael A. Crabb on 16 Mar 1876 in Lone Oak, Hunt County, Texas. She was born on 10 Mar 1853 in Cedertown, Georgia. She died on 16 Feb 1919 in Lone Oak, Hunt County, Texas.

 v. SUSANNAH ELIZABETH PAYNE was born on 13 Jan 1850 in Barren County, Kentucky. She died on 12 Feb 1918.

More About Susannah Elizabeth Payne:
Burial: Hall Cemetery, Lone Oak, Hunt County, Texas
Living In: 1880 Living with her parents in Precinct 4, Hunt County, Texas.
Living In: 1900 Living with her brother, Henry, and his family in Justice Precinct 8, Hunt County, Texas.
Living In: 1910 Living with her sister in law, Mary Frances (wife of Henry Payne) and her family in Justice Precinct 8, Hunt County, Texas.

Notes for Susannah Elizabeth Payne:
Headstone has Susan E. Payne for name.

18. vi. JAMES PAYNE was born on 20 Oct 1851 in Barren County, Kentucky. He died on 04 Jan 1919 in Lone Oak, Texas. He married Martha Evelyn Morris, daughter of Joseph Hubard Morris and Martha Jane Simmons on 20 Oct 1878 in Hunt County, Texas. She was born on 09 Apr 1860 in Lone Oak, Hunt County, Texas. She died on 18 Sep 1929 in Lone Oak, Texas.

19. vii. LEWIS PAYNE was born on 04 Nov 1852 in Barren County, Kentucky. He died on 15 Jan 1930 in Dallas, Dallas County, Texas. He married Frances Ella Scott, daughter of William Lawrence Scott and Elizabeth DeJernett on 24 Jan 1877 in Greenville, Hunt County, Texas. She was born on 08 Jan 1858 in Greenville, Texas. She died on 26 May 1926 in Dallas, Dallas County, Texas.

20. viii. AMELIA MILDRED PAYNE was born on 04 Jan 1857 in Lone Oak, Texas. She died on 15 Nov 1941 in Fort Worth, Tarrant County, Texas. She married Richard Alexander Scott on 11 Jul 1878 in Hunt County, Texas. He was born on 01 Feb 1857 in Anna. Union County, Illinois. He died on 07 May 1931 in Zepher, Brown County, Texas.

21. ix. HENRY PAYNE was born on 23 Nov 1856 in Lone Oak, Texas. He died on 26 Oct 1903 in Lone Oak, Texas. He married Mary Frances Slemmons, daughter of William Washington Slemmons and Susan Elizabeth Glass on 08 Mar 1883 in Lone Oak, Texas. She was born on 08 Jan 1867 in Glasgow, Barren County, Kentucky. She died on 30 Jul 1934 in Lubbock, Texas.

22. x. MARY KATHERINE PAYNE was born on 01 Sep 1858 in Lone Oak, Texas. She married (1) JOSEPH THOMAS WILLIAMS, son of William M. Williams and Anna Jones on 16 Dec 1874 in Hunt County, Texas. He was born on 16 Oct 1853 in Texas. He died on 03 Apr 1923 in Dallas, Dallas County, Texas. She married (2) WILLIAM ASBERRY BRIDGES, son of Pierce Bridges and Harriett Clifton between 03 Apr 1923-02 Apr 1930. He was born on 15 Jan 1860 in Hopkins County, Texas. He died on 03 Dec 1936 in Precinct 4, Hunt County, Texas.

23.   xi. NATHAN PAYNE was born on 14 Aug 1860 in Lone Oak, Texas. He died on 22 Jul 1927 in Fort Worth, Texas. He married Martha Jane Holt on 25 Sep 1881 in Hunt County, Texas. She was born on 18 Sep 1863 in Savannah, Tennessee. She died on 09 Sep 1938 in Fort Worth, Tarrant County, Texas.

          xii. NANCY DORA PAYNE was born on 08 Jun 1863 in Lone Oak, Texas. She died on 24 Jul 1866 in Lone Oak, Texas.

14.   **VINCENT S.**[5] **PAYNE** (Edmund[4], Reuben[3], Thomas[2], Thomas[1]) was born in 1819 in Barren County, Kentucky. He died in 1865 in Hunt County, Texas. He married Mildred Glass, daughter of Benjamin Glass and Susanna Franklin on 13 Jan 1842 in Glasgow, Barren County, Kentucky. She was born on 02 Apr 1827 in Barren County. Kentucky. She died on 28 Oct 1883 in Hunt County, Texas.

More About Vincent S. Payne:
Occupation: 1850 in Division 2, Barren County, Kentucky; Farmer
Occupation: 1860 in Beat 4, Hunt County, Texas; Farmer
Military Service: Bet. 12 Sep-31 Dec 1863 in Greenville, Hunt County, Texas; Enlisted in Company E, 2nd Cavalry, Texas State Troops, C.S.A.
Military Service: 12 Dec 1863; Enlisted in Texas "Brush Battalion", C.S.A., at Bonham, Texas.
Property: 1860 in Hunt County, Texas; 70 Acres Improved and 1230 Acres Unimproved

Notes for Vincent S. Payne:
1865 death date given by daughter of Jesse Marie Mason.

Vincent Payne is alleged to have been a member of the John Honeycutt expedition, a small group of Hunt County men who left Confederate Army service in late 1864 or early 1865 and are thought to have been on their way to Mexico. None of the men were ever seen or heard from again.

More About Mildred Glass:
b: Abt. 1826
Burial: East Mount Cemetery, Greenville, Hunt County, Texas
Living In: 1880 Divorced and living with sons William and George in the home of her son in law, R.A. Hill, in Precinct 1, Hunt County, Texas.

Vincent S. Payne and Mildred Glass had the following children:

24.   i. SUSAN M.[6] PAYNE was born about 1843 in Kentucky. She died after 04 Jun 1880. She married (1) JOSEPH L. ROBY on 20 Oct 1859 in Hunt County, Texas. He was born about 1835 in Ohio. She married (2) OTIS H. BURTON about 1864. He was born about 1840 in Maine.

          ii. JAMES W. PAYNE was born in 1846 in Kentucky.

          iii. BENJAMIN F. PAYNE was born in 1847 in Kentucky.

          iv. NANCY E. PAYNE was born about 1848 in Kentucky.

          v. WILLIAM H. PAYNE was born in 1850 in Kentucky.

              More About William H. Payne:
              Living In: 1870 Living with his younger siblings next door to his mother and step father in Precinct 1, Hunt County, Texas.
              Living In: 1880 Living in the home of his brother in law, R.A. Hill, in Precinct 1,

Hunt County, Texas.

    vi.   WILSON PAYNE was born in 1853 in Kentucky. He died in 1874.

        More About Wilson Payne:
        Living In: 1870 Living with his brother, William, next door to his mother and step father in Precinct 1, Hunt County, Texas.

25.   vii. CATHARINE PAYNE was born on 19 Feb 1854 in Barren County, Kentucky. She died on 08 Jun 1910. She married (1) ROBERT A. HILL on 19 Feb 1873 in Hunt County, Texas. He was born about 1846 in Virginia. She married (2) JAMES E. HORNE on 03 Oct 1894 in Hunt County, Texas. He was born on 03 May 1849 in Mississippi. He died on 27 May 1929 in Dallas, Dallas County, Texas.

    viii. ALONZO PAYNE was born on 10 Oct 1855 in Barren County, Kentucky.

26.   ix. GEORGE VINSON PAYNE was born on 10 Sep 1858 in Texas. He died on 29 Mar 1955 in Dallas, Dallas County, Texas. He married Edith Gorman, daughter of Felix Gorman and Mary A. (unknown) on 26 Aug 1888 in Hunt County, Texas. She was born on 22 Feb 1864 in Texas. She died on 29 Oct 1935.

27.   x.   ALFLEETA PAYNE was born on 18 Nov 1863 in Hunt County, Texas. She died on 17 Nov 1939 in Greenville, Hunt County, Texas. She married Jesse Mason on 13 Sep 1877 in Hopkins County, Texas. He was born on 22 Jul 1845 in Indiana. He died on 19 Sep 1914.

Generation 6

15. **WILLIAM**[6] **PAYNE** (Nathan[5], Edmund[4], Reuben[3], Thomas[2], Thomas[1]) was born on 06 Nov 1842 in Barren County, Kentucky. He died on 02 Nov 1909 in Denton, Texas. He married Mary Francis Weatherly, daughter of Augustus Graham Weatherly and Elizabeth Jane Harrison on 06 Dec 1865 in Hunt County, Texas. She was born on 19 Sep 1848 in Paulding County, Georgia. She died on 10 Apr 1915 in Denton, Texas.

More About William Payne:
Burial: Odd Fellows Cemetery, Denton, Texas
Living In: 1850 Barren County, Kentucky
Living In: 1860 Hunt County, Texas
Occupation: 1870 in Precinct 4, Hunt County, Texas; Farmer
Occupation: 1880 in Precinct 4, Hunt County, Texas; Farmer
Occupation: 1900 in Whitewright, Grayson County, Texas; Landlord
Occupation: Mayor of Whitewright, Texas
Military Service: Soldier C.S.A.

Notes for William Payne:
Will dated September 9, 1902.
Will filed November 4, 1909.
Application for Probate of Will, County Court of Denton County, Texas, January term 1910.

More About Mary Francis Weatherly:
Burial: Odd Fellows Cemetery, Denton, Texas

Living In: 1910 Denton, Denton County, Texas

Notes for Mary Francis Weatherly:
Francis is the correct spelling for Mary's middle name.

William Payne and Mary Francis Weatherly had the following children:

28.   i. FLORA BELLE[7] PAYNE was born on 15 Dec 1868 in Lone Oak, Texas. She died on 30 Dec 1938 in Sherman, Texas. She married (1) CHARLES EDWARD SAVAGE, son of Edward William Savage and Martha Jane Trussell on 15 Feb 1893 in Grayson County, Texas. He was born on 10 Jan 1867 in Grenada, Mississippi. He died on 1 Mar 1919 in Sherman, Texas. She married (2) WILLIAM HICKS BRAY, son of James Bray and Mary Wilson on 11 Sep 1934 in Clay County, Texas. He was born on 08 Jan 1868 in Texas. He died on 14 May 1941 in Lubbock, Texas.

29.   ii. MARY ELIZABETH PAYNE was born on 04 Nov 1866 in Lone Oak, Texas. She died on 23 Jan 1957 in University Park, Dallas County, Texas. She married Charles W. Melson on 29 Feb 1888 in Hunt County, Texas. He was born on 06 Oct 1860 in Missouri. He died on 21 Sep 1925 in Floydada, Floyd County, Texas.

30.   iii. WILLIAM EMMET PAYNE was born on 10 Feb 1872 in Texas. He died on 07 Feb 1920 in Gainsville, Texas. He married HATTIE ANN BURT. She was born on 22 Dec 1896 in Arkansas. She died on 25 Aug 1976 in Plainview, Hale County, Texas.

31.   iv. LESLIE NEWTON PAYNE was born on 14 Jun 1874 in Texas. He died on 16 Apr 1932 in Gainesville, Cooke County, Texas. He married Lela Belle Biffle, daughter of J. T. Biffle and Mary Jane Brown on 01 May 1901 in Cooke County, Texas. She was born on 05 Oct 1882 in Myra, Cooke County, Texas. She died on 23 Dec 1948 in Myra, Cooke County, Texas.

32.   v. METTIE KATHRYN PAYNE was born on 04 Dec 1877 in Texas. She died on 14 Apr 1947 in Fort Worth, Tarrant County, Texas. She married Marion Pace, son of W. A. Pace and Sarah Hawkins after 30 May 1912. He was born on 11 Jul 1852 in Indiana. He died on 17 Jul 1930 in Cleburne, Johnson County, Texas.

33.   vi. FRANCES EDITH PAYNE was born on 18 Dec 1880 in Lone Oak, Texas. She died on 4 Jan 1957 in University Park, Dallas County, Texas. She married JOSEPH NELSON FENDER. He was born on 02 Jan 1877 in Kaufman County, Texas. He died on 28 Nov 1967 in Dallas, Dallas County, Texas.

    viii. GRAHAM LEWIS PAYNE was born on 09 Mar 1883 in Texas. He died on 14 Apr 1951 in Dallas, Dallas County, Texas. He married MADELEINE ROSE MADDEN. She was born on 24 Nov 1892 in Texas. She died on 12 May 1976 in Dallas, Dallas County, Texas.

    More About Graham Lewis Payne:
    Burial: Odd Fellows Cemetery, Denton, Denton County, Texas Cause Of Death: Acute Myocardial Infarction
    Occupation: 1910 in Fort Worth, Tarrant County, Texas; Manager of Tailoring Company
    Occupation: 1920 in Dallas, Dallas County, Texas; Shoe Company Salesman
    Occupation: 1930 in Dallas, Dallas County, Texas; Jobber at Wholesale House
    Occupation: 1940 in Preston Hollow, Dallas County, Texas; Manufacturer with Underwear Factory
    Occupation: 1951 in Dallas, Dallas County, Texas; Proprietor of Garment Factory

Notes for Graham Lewis Payne:
No Issue.

16.   **EDMUND**[6] **PAYNE** (Nathan[5], Edmund[4], Reuben[3], Thomas[2], Thomas[1]) was born on 29 Jun 1846 in Barren County, Kentucky. He died on 22 May 1919. He married Mary Virginia Harrison, daughter of John Harrison and Rhoda Gordon on 27 Mar 1867 in Hunt County, Texas. She was born on 05 Jan 1850 in Georgia. She died on 27 Apr 1929.

More About Edmund Payne:
Burial: Rose Hill Cemetery, Wapanucka, Johnston County, Oklahoma
Occupation: 1870 in Precinct 4, Hunt County, Texas; Farmer
Occupation: 1880 in Precinct 4, Hunt County, Texas; Farmer
Occupation: 1910 in Caddo, Bryan County, Oklahoma; City Police Man

More About Mary Virginia Harrison:
Burial: Rose Hill Cemetery, Wapanucka, Johnston County, Oklahoma
Living In: 1920 Living with her daughter, Mary, and her daughter's husband in Ada, Pontotoc County, Oklahoma.

More About Edmund Payne and Mary Virginia Harrison:
m: 1867

Edmund Payne and Mary Virginia Harrison had the following children:

      i.   ALEXANDER LEE[7] PAYNE was born on 28 Sep 1868 in Lone Oak, Texas. He died in 1929. He married D. LEOTA. He married JOSE MEDLIN.

      ii.   MARY SUE PAYNE was born on 21 Dec 1870. She married ORLANDO R. NANCE. He was born about 1868 in Tennessee. She married O. R. NANCE.

More About Mary Sue Payne:
Occupation: 1920 in Ada, Pontotoc County, Oklahoma; Department Store Saleslady

      iii.   NANCY MILDRED PAYNE was born on 13 Jul 1873 in Lone Oak, Texas. She died on 4 Sep 1888.

      iv.   ZORA AMANDA PAYNE was born on 15 Dec 1875 in Lone Oak, Texas. She died on 8 Jul 1938 in Dallas, Dallas County, Texas. She married EDWARD THEODORE HAMER.

      v.   BENJAMIN HOUSTON PAYNE was born on 28 Jul 1878 in Lone Oak, Texas. He died on 01 Jun 1957. He married LILLIE MAE CROSSETT.

      vi.   EDDIE LOU PAYNE was born on 24 Jun 1882.

17.   **ANDREW ALEXANDER**[6] **PAYNE** (Nathan[5], Edmund[4], Reuben[3], Thomas[2], Thomas[1]) was born on 09 May 1848 in Barren County, Kentucky. He died on 07 Oct 1920 in Lone Oak, Hunt County, Texas. He married Carrie Weatherly, daughter of Isaac C. Weatherly and Rachael A. Crabb on 16 Mar 1876 in Lone Oak, Hunt County, Texas. She was born on 10 Mar 1853 in Cedertown, Georgia. She died on 16 Feb 1919 in Lone Oak, Hunt County, Texas.

More About Andrew Alexander Payne:
Burial: Lone Oak Cemetery, Hunt County, Texas
Living In: 1870 Living with his parents in Precinct 4, Hunt County, Texas.
Occupation: 1870 in Hunt County, Texas; Farm Labor
Occupation: 1880 in Precinct 4, Hunt County, Texas; Farmer
Occupation: 1900 in Lone Oak, Hunt County, Texas; Farmer
Occupation: 1910 in Lone Oak, Hunt County, Texas; City Mayor
Occupation: Hunt County, Texas; Justice of the Peace

More About Carrie Weatherly:
Burial: 17 Feb 1919 in Lone Oak Cemetery, Hunt County, Texas

Notes for Carrie Weatherly:
Funeral conducted by Reverend J. A. Roper.

Andrew Alexander Payne and Carrie Weatherly had the following children:

    i.   FLORENCE[7] PAYNE was born in Aug 1877 in Texas. She married J. V. NASH.

    ii.   ALMA R. PAYNE was born on 20 Jan 1879 in Lone Oak, Texas. She died on 26 Feb 1941 in Lone Oak, Hunt County, Texas. She married (1) FRANK N. BRYAN on 12 Jun 1895 in Lone Oak, Texas. He was born on 19 Mar 1875. He died on 18 Oct 1895 in Lone Oak, Hunt County, Texas. She married (2) WILLIAM C. DOWELL on 09 Aug 1898 in Lone Oak, Texas. He was born in Nov 1871 in Texas. He died in 1938 in Lone Oak, Hunt County, Texas.

    More About Alma R. Payne:
    Burial: 27 Feb 1941 in Lone Oak Cemetery, Hunt County, Texas
    Occupation: Bet. 1938-1940 ; Acting Postmaster of Lone Oak, Texas.

    Notes for Alma R. Payne:
    Fureral Service conducted by Dr. C. B. Jackson, Pastor of the First Baptist Church of Greenville.

    iii.   NENA E. PAYNE was born in Jul 1885 in Lone Oak, Hunt County, Texas. She died in 1961 in Lone Oak, Hunt County, Texas. She married James V. Nash on 01 May 1904 in Lone Oak, Texas. He was born on 30 Jun 1877 in Texas. He died on 19 Jan 1938 in Lone Oak, Hunt County, Texas.

34.   iv. FLOYD ALEXANDER PAYNE was born on 15 May 1888 in Lone Oak, Hunt County, Texas. He died on 16 Sep 1966 in San Angelo, Texas. He married WILLIE WALSH. She was born in 1892 in Texas.

18.   JAMES[6] PAYNE (Nathan[5], Edmund[4], Reuben[3], Thomas[2], Thomas[1]) was born on 20 Oct 1851 in Barren County, Kentucky. He died on 04 Jan 1919 in Lone Oak, Texas. He married Martha Evelyn Morris, daughter of Joseph Hubard Morris and Martha Jane Simmons on 20 Oct 1878 in Hunt County, Texas. She was born on 09 Apr 1860 in Lone Oak, Hunt County, Texas. She died on 18 Sep 1929 in Lone Oak, Texas.

More About James Payne:
Burial: Hall Cemetery, Lone Oak, Hunt County, Texas
Occupation: 1880 in Precinct 4, Hunt County, Texas; Farmer
Occupation: 1900 in Justice Precinct 8, Hunt County, Texas; Farmer

Occupation: 1910 in Justice Precinct 8, Hunt County, Texas; Farmer

More About Martha Evelyn Morris:
Burial: 19 Sep 1929 in Hall Cemetery, Lone Oak, Hunt County, Texas
Living In: 1920 Living in Lone Oak, Hunt County, Texas with her children, James and Vera.

Notes for Martha Evelyn Morris:
1929 - 19 Sep 1929 - Greenville Morning Herald, p.
1: MRS PAYNE
PASSES AWAY
Well-Known Resident Lone Oak
Dies in Local Hospital Wednesday

Mrs. Mattie Payne, 69 years of age, prominent resident of the Lone Oak community for more than three score years, died at a local hospital at 9:30 0'clock Wednesday morning following an operation.
Mrs. Payne was born and reared in Hunt County and resided in the Lone Oak community nearly all her years. She united with the Methodist Church at an early age and lived a consistent Christian life.
She is survived by ten children: Olie {Olive}, Nathan, Cecil, Lena, Locket, Joe, Lester{Luster}, Jimmie, Ivie, and Vera, and also one sister and three brothers. Her husband preceded her in death in 1919.
Funeral services will be held at 2:30 o'clock this afternoon from Lone Oak Methodist Church, with interment following in the Hall Cemetery.

James Payne and Martha Evelyn Morris had the following children:

    i.   OLIVE[7] PAYNE was born about Jan 1880 in Texas.

    ii.   NATHAN PAYNE was born in Sep 1881 in Texas.

    iii.   CECIL PAYNE was born in Dec 1883 in Texas.

    iv.   EVA PAYNE was born about Oct 1885. She died on 24 Oct 1886.

    More About Eva Payne:
    Burial: Hall Cemetery, Lone Oak, Texas

    v.   LENA PAYNE was born in Mar 1887 in Texas.

    vi.   LOCKET PAYNE was born in Dec 1888 in Texas.

    vii.   JOSEPH PAYNE was born in Aug 1890 in Texas.

    viii.   LESTER PAYNE was born on 16 Jul 1893 in Lone Oak, Hunt County, Texas. He died on 05 Jul 1951 in Lone Oak, Hunt County, Texas.

    ix.   JAMES PAYNE was born in Feb 1895 in Texas.

    x.   IDA PAYNE was born in Dec 1896 in Texas.

xi.   VERA PAYNE was born on 10 Jun 1900 in Texas. She died on 26 Jan 1948.

More About Vera Payne:
Burial: Hall Cemetery, Lone Oak, Hunt County, Texas

19.   LEWIS[6] PAYNE (Nathan[5], Edmund[4], Reuben[3], Thomas[2], Thomas[1]) was born on 04 Nov 1852 in Barren County, Kentucky. He died on 15 Jan 1930 in Dallas, Dallas County, Texas. He married Frances Ella Scott, daughter of William Lawrence Scott and Elizabeth DeJernett on 24 Jan 1877 in Greenville, Hunt County, Texas. She was born on 08 Jan 1858 in Greenville, Texas. She died on 26 May 1926 in Dallas, Dallas County, Texas.

More About Lewis Payne:
Burial: 16 Jan 1930 in Forest Park Cemetery, Greenville,
Texas Cause Of Death: Pneumonia
Occupation: 1880 in Precinct 4, Hunt County, Texas; Deputy Sheriff.
Occupation: 1900 in Greenville, Hunt County, Texas; Grocer (store was called "Payne and Long")
Occupation: 1910 in Greenville, Hunt County, Texas; County Treasurer
Occupation: 1920 in Greenville, Hunt County, Texas; Retired

Notes for Lewis Payne:
Owned Long and Payne Grocery Store in Greenville, Texas.

More About Frances Ella Scott:
Burial: 27 May 1926 in Forest Park Cemetery, Greenville, Texas
Cause Of Death: Brights Disease

Notes for Frances Ella Scott:
Death certificate gives date of birth as January 8, 1858. Headstone gives date of birth as January 8, 1855.

Lewis Payne and Frances Ella Scott had the following children:
i.   WILLIE PEARL[7] PAYNE was born in Jan 1879 in Texas. She married (UNKNOWN) HOWELL.

More About Willie Pearl Payne:
Living In: 1920 Willie and her daughter are living with her parents in Greenville, Hunt County, Texas.
Occupation: 1920 in Greenville, Hunt County, Texas; Book Keeper for Cotton Company

Notes for Willie Pearl Payne:
Widow before January 7, 1920.

ii.   MARY MUADE PAYNE was born in Oct 1880 in Texas. She married WILLIAM W. ALSOBROOK. He was born about 1861 in Tennessee.

More About Mary Muade Payne:
Living In: 1910 Mary and her husband are living with her parents in Greenville, Hunt County, Texas.

     iii.   OPAL ELIZABETH PAYNE was born in Dec 1884 in Texas. She married BENTON HUCKABAY. He was born about 1876 in Texas.

         More About Opal Elizabeth Payne:
Living In: 1910 Elizabeth and her husband are living with her parents in Greenville, Hunt County, Texas.

     iv.   ELLA MAY PAYNE was born in Apr 1892 in Texas.

     v.   LEWIS PAYNE.

20.   **AMELIA MILDRED[6] PAYNE** (Nathan[5], Edmund[4], Reuben[3], Thomas[2], Thomas[1]) was born on 04 Jan 1857 in Lone Oak, Texas. She died on 15 Nov 1941 in Fort Worth, Tarrant County, Texas. She married Richard Alexander Scott on 11 Jul 1878 in Hunt County, Texas. He was born on 01 Feb 1857 in Anna. Union County, Illinois. He died on 07 May 1931 in Zepher, Brown County, Texas.

More About Amelia Mildred Payne:
Burial: 17 Nov 1941 in Greenwood Memorial Park, Fort Worth, Tarrant County,
Texas Cause Of Death: ; Bronchial Pneumonia
Living In: 1900 Divorced and living with Willie and Beryl in Lone Oak, Hunt County, Texas
Living In: 1910 Living with her daughter, Beryl, and Beryl's husband in Fort Worth, Tarrant County, Texas.
Living In: 1930 Living with her daughter, Beryl, and Beryl's daughter, Opal, in Fort Worth, Tarrant County, Texas.
Living In: 1940 Living with her daughter, Beryl, and Beryl's daughter, Opal, in Fort Worth, Tarrant County, Texas.

Notes for Amelia Mildred Payne:
Date of birth is from death certificate information provided by her daughter, Beryl.

More About Richard Alexander Scott:
Burial: 09 May 1931 in Zepher Cemetery, Zepher, Brown County,
Texas
Cause Of Death: Pneumonia
Occupation: 1880 in Precinct 4, Hunt County, Texas; Farmer

Richard Alexander Scott and Amelia Mildred Payne had the following children:

35.   i. BERYL[7] SCOTT was born on 08 Mar 1889 in Lone Oak, Hunt County, Texas. She died on 24 Jun 1965 in Fort Worth, Tarrant County, Texas. She married J. H. WRIGHT. He was born about 1885 in Missouri.

     ii. WILLIE SCOTT was born in Jun 1885 in Texas.

     iii. AURA SCOTT was born on 06 Mar 1879 in Texas. She died on 25 Nov 1900. She married Zacharias Edmond Gandy on 18 Oct 1898 in Hunt County, Texas. He was born on 24 Feb 1879 in Hunt County, Texas. He died on 27 Dec 1964 in Arlington, Tarrant County, Texas.

         More About Aura Scott:
Burial: Lone Oak Cemetery, Lone Oak, Hunt County, Texas

21.   **HENRY[6] PAYNE** (Nathan[5], Edmund[4], Reuben[3], Thomas[2], Thomas[1]) was born on 23 Nov 1856 in

Lone Oak, Texas. He died on 26 Oct 1903 in Lone Oak, Texas. He married Mary Frances Slemmons, daughter of William Washington Slemmons and Susan Elizabeth Glass on 08 Mar 1883 in Lone Oak, Texas. She was born on 08 Jan 1867 in Glasgow, Barren County, Kentucky. She died on 30 Jul 1934 in Lubbock, Texas.

More About Henry Payne:
Burial: Lone Oak Cemetery, Hunt County,
Texas
Cause Of Death: Small Pox
Living In: 1880 Living with his parents in Precinct 4, Hunt County, Texas.
Occupation: 1900 in Justice Precinct 8, Hunt County, Texas; Farmer

More About Mary Frances Slemmons:
Burial: Lone Oak Cemetery, Hunt County, Texas
Living In: 1910 Mary and her chilldren are living in Justce Precinct 8, Hunt County, Texas.
Living In: 1920 Living with her son, Lewis, in Justice Precinct 8, Hunt County, Texas.
Occupation: 1910 in Justice Precinct 8, Hunt County, Texas; Farmer
Occupation: 1930 in Precinct 8, Hunt County, Texas; Farmer

Notes for Mary Frances Slemmons:
1934 - Tuesday, 31 Jul 1934 - Greenville Evening Banner:

Lone Oak Woman
 Died in Lubbock

Mrs. Mary F. Payne, 67, long time resident of the Lone Oak community passed away last night about 9 0'clock at the home of her son, Nathan Payne in Lubbock where she was visiting. The body will be brought to this city and will arrive late night or early tomorrow and will be carried direct to Lone Oak where funeral arrangements will be made.
 Born in Glasgow, Kentucky on January 8, 1867, Mrs. Payne moved to Texas with her parents when she was a small child and settled in the Lone Oak community. She was married to Henry Payne and they lived north of Lone Oak practically all of their married life.
 She was one of the most beloved women of Lone Oak section and had hundreds of friends who will be grieved to learn of her death. Mrs. Payne was a sister of Mrs. P. C. White of Greenville and often visited this city. She had many friends here who will join the bereaved relatives in mourning her death.
 For years Mrs. Payne had been a member of the Methodist church and had lived true to the teachings of the Master.
 Surviving are the following children: Mrs. Ed. Moxley of Ropes, Texas; John Payne of Spur; Nathan Payne of Lubbock; Miss Sue Payne of Lone Oak; Lewis Payne of Lone Oak; Mrs. Jim Bailey of Lubbock; Mrs. Myrtle Crow of Haskell; Arlon Payne of Lubbock. She is also survived by her 90 year old father, W. W. Slemmons of Lone Oak, two brothers, Lewis Slemmons of Abernathy and John Slemmons of Mineral Wells and three sisters, Mrs. J. C. White of Greenville; Mrs. A. J. Broyles, El Dorado, Okla., and Mrs. J. D. Barton, Amarillo. Several grandchildren and great grandchildren as well as several half brothers and sisters also survive.

Henry Payne and Mary Frances Slemmons had the following children:

36. i. ANICE LOU[7] PAYNE was born on 24 May 1884 in Lone Oak, Texas. She died on 03 Jul 1978 in Andrews, Texas. She married George Edmond Moxley about 1903. He was born in Mar 1884 in Texas. He died on 06 Jan 1965.

37. ii. JOHN CRENSHAW PAYNE was born on 06 Dec 1885 in Lone Oak, Texas. He died on 16 Mar 1958 in Spur, Texas. He married Bessie L. Ensey in 1911. She was born in 1895 in Texas.

38.   iii. NATHAN ALEXANDER PAYNE was born on 31 May 1887 in Lone Oak, Texas. He died on 09
           Aug 1953 in Lubbock, Texas. He married Lillie Mae Jenkins, daughter of Horace
           Jenkins and Mary Fortenberry on 10 Nov 1907 in Lone Oak, Texas. She was born on
           16 Jul 1891 in Lone Oak, Texas. She died on 17 Mar 1963 in Lubbock, Texas.

     iv.   MARY SUSAN PAYNE was born on 31 Aug 1888 in Lone Oak, Texas. She died on
            27 Dec 1978 in Greenville, Texas.

            More About Mary Susan Payne:
            Burial: 29 Dec 1978 in Lone Oak Cemetery, Hunt County,
            Texas Burial:
            Living In: 1910 Living with her mother in Justice Precinct 8, Hunt County, Texas.
            Living In: 1920 Living with her brother, Lewis, in Justice Precinct 8, Hunt County,
            Texas.
            Occupation: 1910 in Justice Precinct 8, Hunt County, Texas; County
            School Teacher
            Occupation: 1920 in Justice Precinct 8, Hunt County, Texas; Public School Teacher

            Notes   for   Mary   Susan
            Payne: Never Married.

     v.   LEWIS REDMOND PAYNE was born on 18 Nov 1889 in Lone Oak, Texas. He died
            on 25 Jun 1953 in Lone Oak, Hunt County, Texas.

            More About Lewis Redmond Payne:
            Burial: Lone Oak Cemetery, Hunt County, Texas
            Living In: 1910 Living with his mother in Justice Precinct 8, Hunt County, Texas.
            Living In: 1930 Living with his mother in Precinct 8, Hunt County, Texas
            Occupation: 1910 in Justice Precinct 8, Hunt County, Texas; Farm Laborer
            Occupation: 1920 in Justice Precinct 8, Hunt County, Texas; Farmer
            Occupation: 1930 in Precinct 8, Hunt County, Texas; Farmer
            Occupation: Stock Farmer
            Military Service: World War One

            Notes for Lewis Redmond Payne:
            Never Married.

39.   vi. CATHERINE ZELMA PAYNE was born on 16 Feb 1894 in Lone Oak, Texas. She died in Dec
           1982. She married Jim Bailey in 1912. He died in 1952.

40.   vii. HENRY YOAKUM PAYNE was born on 08 Jan 1896 in Lone Oak, Texas. He died on
            28 Jun 1921 in Lubbock, Texas. He married Myrtle Ensley on 25 Oct 1917.
            She was born about 1900 in Texas.

     ix.   AMELIA CRISTIAN PAYNE was born on 27 Apr 1897 in Lone Oak, Texas. She died on
            1 May 1991.

            More About Amelia Cristian Payne:
            Living In: 1920 Living with her brother, Lewis, in Justice Precinct 8, Hunt County,
            Texas.

41.   ix. ARLON GODBY PAYNE was born on 03 Apr 1900 in Lone Oak, Texas. He died on 26 Aug 1961 in Harrison, Arkansas. He married NONA MAE ARMSTRONG. She was born on 11 Mar 1899. She died on 28 Oct 1979 in Arkansas.

22.   MARY KATHERINE[6] PAYNE (Nathan[5], Edmund[4], Reuben[3], Thomas[2], Thomas[1]) was born on 01 Sep 1858 in Lone Oak, Texas. She married (1) JOSEPH THOMAS WILLIAMS, son of William M. Williams and Anna Jones on 16 Dec 1874 in Hunt County, Texas. He was born on 16 Oct 1853 in Texas. He died on 03 Apr 1923 in Dallas, Dallas County, Texas. She married (2) WILLIAM ASBERRY BRIDGES, son of Pierce Bridges and Harriett Clifton between 03 Apr 1923-02 Apr 1930. He was born on 15 Jan 1860 in Hopkins County, Texas. He died on 03 Dec 1936 in Precinct 4, Hunt County, Texas.

More About Mary Katherine Payne:
Burial: Williams Chapel Cemetery, Lone Oak, Hunt County, Texas

Notes for Mary Katherine Payne:
Headstone has Mary Katherine's name and birth date but no death date for her.

More About Joseph Thomas Williams:
Burial: Williams Chapel Cemetery, Lone Oak, Hunt County, Texas
Occupation: 1880 in Precinct 4, Hunt County, Texas; Farmer
Occupation: 1900 in Justice Precinct 8, Hunt County, Texas; Farmer
Occupation: 1920 in Justice Precinct 8, Hunt County, Texas; Farm Operator

Notes for Joseph Thomas Williams:
Death certificate has April 3, 1923 for date of death. Headstone has April 2, 1923 for date of death.

Joseph Thomas Williams and Mary Katherine Payne had the following children:

    i.   CHARLIE[7] WILLIAMS was born on 20 Sep 1877. He died on 26 Apr 1878.

        More About Charlie Williams:
        Burial: Rabb Cemetery, Lone Oak, Texas

    ii.   MAY B. WILLIAMS was born in Mar 1879 in Texas.

    iii.   JOSEPH MAXWELL WILLIAMS was born on 24 Apr 1883 in Texas. He died on 18 Nov 1971.

        More About Joseph Maxwell Williams:
        Burial: Oak Hill Burial Park, Lakeland, Polk County, Florida

        Notes for Joseph Maxwell Williams:
        Joseph and Fannie are apparently twins born six days apart.

43.   iv. FANNIE SUE WILLIAMS was born on 30 Apr 1883 in Lone Oak, Hunt County, Texas. She died on 24 Jun 1956 in Greenville, Texas. She married Albert L. Dodd on 29 Nov 1902 in Hunt County, Texas. He was born on 02 Nov 1879 in Texas. He died

on 07 Apr 1961 in Austin, Texas.

    v.   MONNIE ELLEN WILLIAMS was born on 06 Aug 1888 in Lone Oak, Hunt County, Texas. She died on 11 Feb 1959 in Greenville, Hunt County, Texas. She married (UNKNOWN) HULSEY.

    vi.   ANNIE WILLIAMS was born on 22 May 1903 in Texas. She died on 07 Jul 1976 in San Antonio, Bexar County, Texas. She married (UNKNOWN) GAGE.

More About William Asberry Bridges:
Burial: Brigham Cemetery, Campbell, Hunt County, Texas
Occupation: 1930 in Lone Oak, Hunt County, Texas; Monument Salesman

23.   NATHAN[6] PAYNE (Nathan[5], Edmund[4], Reuben[3], Thomas[2], Thomas[1]) was born on 14 Aug 1860 in Lone Oak, Texas. He died on 22 Jul 1927 in Fort Worth, Texas. He married Martha Jane Holt on 25 Sep 1881 in Hunt County, Texas. She was born on 18 Sep 1863 in Savannah, Tennessee. She died on 09 Sep 1938 in Fort Worth, Tarrant County, Texas.

More About Nathan Payne:
Burial: 23 Jul 1927 in Hall Cemetery, Lone Oak, Hunt County, Texas
Occupation: 1900 in Justice Precinct 8, Hunt County, Texas; House Carpenter
Occupation: 1910 in Quanah, Hardeman County, Texas; House Contractor

Notes for Nathan Payne:
1927 - Thursday, 28 Jul 1927 - The Greenville Messenger:

NAT PAYNE DIED
AT FORT WORTH

Nat Payne, aged 67 years and formerly of Lone Oak, died at Ft. Worth last week at the age of 67 years and the body was brought to Lone Oak and burial in the old Hall cemetery just west of that place.
 Deceased was a brother of Lewis Payne of this city and of Mrs. Kate Bridges and Mrs. Mack Scott, of Lone Oak and had many friends among the old timers of that section.
 He is survived by his wife and three daughters: Mrs. John Curlee of Lone Oak; one living in Amarillo and one in Fort Worth.

More About Martha Jane Holt:
Burial: Hall Cemetery, Lone Oak, Hunt County, Texas
Living In: 1920 Fort Worth, Tarrant County, Texas with Grady and Andrew.
Living In: 1930 Fort Worth, Tarrant County, Texas.

Notes for Martha Jane Holt:
On the 1920 U.S. census Martha is listed as a widow although Nathan is still living.

Nathan Payne and Martha Jane Holt had the following children:

    i. ANNIE MYRTLE[7] PAYNE was born on 26 Sep 1884 in Texas. She died on 08 Sep 1954 in Fort Worth, Tarrant County, Texas. She married (UNKNOWN) CURLEE.

More About Annie Myrtle Payne:

Burial: 09 Sep 1954 in Laurel Land Cemetery, Fort worth, Tarrant County, Texas

ii.   EMMA LOU PAYNE was born on 22 Jul 1886. She died on 26 Jul 1887.

More About Emma Lou Payne:
Burial: Hall Cemetery, Lone Oak, Texas

iii.   MARY PEARL PAYNE was born on 09 May 1888 in Texas. She died on 12 Feb 1975 in Fort Worth, Tarrant County, Texas. She married (UNKNOWN) SHEPHERD.

More About Mary Pearl Payne:
Burial: 14 Feb 1975 in Greenwood Memorial Park, Fort Worth, Tarrant County, Texas

iv.   CAPITOLA GRACE PAYNE was born on 13 Jun 1893 in Lone Oak, Hunt County, Texas. She died on 26 Nov 1970 in Fort Worth, Tarrant County, Texas. She married (UNKNOWN) ALDRICH.

More About Capitola Grace Payne:
Burial: 28 Nov 1970 in Laurel Land Cemetery, Fort worth, Tarrant County, Texas

v.   HENRY GRADY PAYNE was born on 13 Jun 1893 in Texas. He died on 07 Oct 1977 in Fort Worth, Tarrant County, Texas.

More About Henry Grady Payne:
Burial: 10 Oct 1977 in Greenwood Memorial Park, Fort Worth, Tarrant County, Texas
Living In: 1920 living with his mother in Fort Worth, Tarrant County, Texas.
Occupation: Vice President of Plumbing Supply Company
Military Service: World War One

43.   vi. NATHAN ORAL PAYNE was born on 08 Mar 1896 in Lone Oak, Hunt County, Texas. He died on 28 Jul 1969 in Burnsville community, Sebastion County, Arkansas. He married NELLIE OWEN. She was born on 11 Sep 1898 in Texas. She died on 13 Feb 1976 in Fort Smith, Arkansas.

vii.   ANDREW JACKSON PAYNE was born on 17 Apr 1900 in Lone Oak, Texas. He died on 27 Apr 1929 in Fort Worth, Texas. He married Harriett Stewart on 17 Apr 1929 in Collin County, Texas. She died on 27 Apr 1929 in Fort Worth, Texas.

More About Andrew Jackson Payne:
Burial: Hall Cemetery, Lone Oak, Texas
Cause Of Death: Three bullet wounds in his chest.
Occupation: Railroad Employee

Notes for Andrew Jackson Payne:

The Greenville Morning Herald, 28 Apr 1929, copied from microfilm of original in William Walworth Public Library in Greenville, Hunt Co., TX:

COUPLE DEAD
DUAL SHOOTING
-
A. J. PAYNE AND BRIDE OF
TEN DAYS ARE DEAD
AT FORT WORTH
-
By The Associated Press.
Fort Worth, April 27. - A.J. Payne and his wife of ten days, Mrs. Harriet
Payne are dead as the result of a double shooting in their apartment here
Saturday night. Payne was dead when police, summoned by neighbors,
broke into the apartment. Mrs. Payne died a few hours later in a hospital.
Neighbors heard several shots fired and called police. The couple were
found lying close together, with a small automatic pistol lying near them.
Payne was dead, with three bullet wounds in his chest. Mrs. Payne was
suffering from one bullet wound in her abdomen.
The wounded woman was taken to a hospital, where she died. Efforts
of officers to take a statement from her to clear up the tragedy were
unsuccessful.

----

24. **SUSAN M.**[6] **PAYNE** (Vincent S.[5], Edmund[4], Reuben[3], Thomas[2], Thomas[1]) was born about 1843
in Kentucky. She died after 04 Jun 1880. She married (1) **JOSEPH L. ROBY** on 20 Oct 1859 in
Hunt County, Texas. He was born about 1835 in Ohio. She married (2) **OTIS H. BURTON** about
1864. He was born about 1840 in Maine.

More About Susan M. Payne:
Living In: 1870 Susan, as Susan Burton, and her daughter, Mildred Roby, are living in Precinct
1, Hunt County, Texas.

Notes for Susan M. Payne:
In 1870 Susan is living next door to her siblings, William, Wilson, George and Alfleeta, and
two doors away from her mother and step father.

More About Joseph L. Roby:
Occupation: 1860 in Beat 4, Hunt County, Texas; Farmer

Joseph L. Roby and Susan M. Payne had the following children:

    i.   VINCENT[7] ROBY was born in 1861.

    ii.   MILDRED ROBY was born about 1865 in Texas. She married (UNKNOWN) HUNNICUT.

        More About Mildred Roby:
        Living In: 1880 Living with her mother and step father in Precinct 1, Hunt County,
        Texas.

More About Otis H. Burton:
Occupation: 1880 in Precinct 1, Hunt County, Texas; Farmer

Otis H. Burton and Susan M. Payne had the following children:

     i.   VIRGINIA[7] BURTON was born about 1873 in Texas.

     ii.   DELLA BURTON was born about 1875 in Texas.

     iii.   OTIS BURTON was born about 1876 in Texas.

     iv.   MARCUS BURTON was born about 1878 in Texas.

25.   **CATHARINE[6] PAYNE** (Vincent S.[5], Edmund[4], Reuben[3], Thomas[2], Thomas[1]) was born on 19 Feb 1854 in Barren County, Kentucky. She died on 08 Jun 1910. She married (1) **ROBERT A. HILL** on 19 Feb 1873 in Hunt County, Texas. He was born about 1846 in Virginia. She married (2) **JAMES E. HORNE** on 03 Oct 1894 in Hunt County, Texas. He was born on 03 May 1849 in Mississippi. He died on 27 May 1929 in Dallas, Dallas County, Texas.

More About Catharine Payne:
Burial: Forest Park Cemetery, Greenville, Hunt County, Texas
Living In: 1870 Living with her brother, William, next door to her mother and step father in Precinct 1, Hunt County, Texas.

Notes for Catharine Payne:
Kentucky birth record has date of birth as February 19, 1854. Headstone has date of birth as February 19, 1856.

More About Robert A. Hill:
Occupation: 1870 in Fort Coucho, Bexar County, Texas; Private in Company B, 11th Infantry, U.S.Army
Occupation: 1880 in Precinct 1, Hunt County, Texas; Sewing Machine Agent
Military Service: 1870 in Fort Coucho, Bexar County, Texas; Company B, 11th Infantry, U.S. Army

Robert A. Hill and Catharine Payne had the following children:

     i.   JESSIE[7] HILL was born about 1877 in Texas.

     ii.   GEORGIE HILL was born about 1879 in Texas.

            More About Georgie Hill:
            Living In: 1900 Living with her mother and step father in Justice Precinct 1, Hunt County, Texas

More About James E. Horne:
Burial: 28 May 1929 in Forest Park Cemetery, Greenville, Hunt County, Texas
Living In: 1929 Greenville, Hunt County, Texas
Occupation: 1900 in Justice Precinct 1, Hunt County, Texas; Farmer and Stock Raiser
Occupation: 1910 in Justice Precinct 1, Hunt County, Texas; Farmer
Occupation: 1920 in Justice Precinct 3, Hunt County, Texas; Salesman in Grocery Store

James E. Horne and Catharine Payne had the following child:

     i.   JAMES E.[7] HORNE was born in Feb 1899 in Texas.

26.   **GEORGE VINSON[6] PAYNE** (Vincent S.[5], Edmund[4], Reuben[3], Thomas[2], Thomas[1]) was born on 10 Sep 1858 in Texas. He died on 29 Mar 1955 in Dallas, Dallas County, Texas. He married Edith Gorman, daughter of Felix Gorman and Mary A. (unknown) on 26 Aug 1888 in Hunt County,

Texas. She was born on 22 Feb 1864 in Texas. She died on 29 Oct 1935.

More About George Vinson Payne:
Burial: 31 Mar 1955 in East Mount Cemetery, Greenville,
Texas
Cause Of Death: Myocardial Infarction
Living In: 1870 Living with his brother, William, next door to his mother and step father in
Precinct 1, Hunt County, Texas.
Living In: 1880 Living in the home of his brother in law, R.A. Hill, in Precinct 1, Hunt County,
Texas.
Occupation: 1900 in Greenville, Hunt County, Texas; Real Estate Dealer
Occupation: 1910 in Dewey, Washington County, Oklahoma; Carpenter Shop
Employee
Occupation: 1920 in Dewey, Washington County, Oklahoma; House Carpenter
Occupation: 1930 in Norman, Cleveland County, Oklahoma; Grocery Store Manager
Occupation: Retail Grocer

Notes for George Vinson Payne:
Death certificate has his middle name as Vinson but Vincent seems more likely.

More About Edith Gorman:
Burial: East Mount Cemetery, Greeneville, Hunt County, Texas

George Vinson Payne and Edith Gorman had the following children:

     i.   WOODWARD[7] PAYNE was born in Aug 1889 in Texas.

     ii.   MILDRED PAYNE was born in Nov 1891 in Texas.

     iii.   LAURA PAYNE was born in Oct 1894 in Texas.

     iv.   FELIX VINCENT PAYNE was born on 19 Jul 1899 in Texas.

27.   ALFLEETA[6] PAYNE (Vincent S.[5], Edmund[4], Reuben[3], Thomas[2], Thomas[1]) was born on 18 Nov 1863 in
Hunt County, Texas. She died on 17 Nov 1939 in Greenville, Hunt County, Texas. She married Jesse
Mason on 13 Sep 1877 in Hopkins County, Texas. He was born on 22 Jul 1845 in Indiana.
He died on 19 Sep 1914.

More About Alfleeta Payne:

b: 18 Nov 1863
Burial: 18 Nov 1939 in East Mount Cemetery, Greenville, Hunt County, Texas
Living In: 1870 Living with her brother, William, next door to her mother and step father in
Precinct 1, Hunt County, Texas.
Living In: 1916 Greenville, Hunt County, Texas

Notes for Alfleeta Payne:
Headstone has November 18, 1863 as date of birth. Death certificate has November 19, 1863
as date of birth.

More About Jesse Mason:
Burial: Greenville, Texas
Burial: East Mount Cemetery, Greenville, Hunt County, Texas
Occupation: 1880 in Precinct 1, Hunt County, Texas; Sewing Machine Agent
Occupation: 1900 in Greenville, Hunt County, Texas; Farmer
Occupation: 1910 in Greenville, Hunt County, Texas; Rail Road Laborer

Jesse Mason and Alfleeta Payne had the following children:

 i. ROBERT[7] MASON was born about Sep 1879 in Texas.

 ii. JESSE MARIE MASON was born on 27 May 1881 in Greenville, Hunt County, Texas. She died on 26 Nov 1949 in Corsicana, Navarro County, Texas. She married Herbert Spencer on 23 Jul 1905.

 More About Jesse Marie Mason:
 Burial: 27 Nov 1949 in Oakwood Cemetery, Corsicana, Navarro County, Texas

 iii. GEORGE M. MASON was born on 25 Sep 1883 in Greenville, Hunt County, Texas. He died on 23 Nov 1969 in Denison, Grayson County, Texas. He married VIOLA ENNIS FINLEY. She was born on 13 Feb 1887. She died on 15 Sep 1958.

 More About George M. Mason:
 Burial: Crown Hill Memorial Park, Dallas, Dallas County, Texas

 iv. DUGAL CONROY MASON was born on 10 Feb 1890 in Texas. He died on 04 Sep 1966 in Austin, Travis County, Texas.

 More About Dugal Conroy Mason:
 Burial: 06 Sep 1966 in Capital Memorial Gardens, Travis County, Texas
 Living In: 1966 Greenville, Hunt County, Texas
 Occupation: Printer

 Notes for Dugal Conroy Mason: Never Married

 v. ALFLEETA M. MASON was born on 01 Jul 1895 in Texas. She died on 24 Nov 1971 in Kerrville, Kerr County, Texas.

 More About Alfleeta M. Mason:
 Burial: 27 Nov 1971 in Garden of Memories, Kerrville, Kerr County, Texas
 Occupation: Public School Teacher

 vi. BERTRAN W. MASON was born on 24 Jun 1898 in Greenville, Hunt County, Texas. He died on 05 Jan 1970 in Greenville, Hunt County, Texas.

Generation 7

28. FLORA BELLE[7] PAYNE (William[6], Nathan[5], Edmund[4], Reuben[3], Thomas[2], Thomas[1]) was born on 15 Dec 1868 in Lone Oak, Texas. She died on 30 Dec 1938 in Sherman, Texas. She married (1) CHARLES EDWARD SAVAGE, son of Edward William Savage and Martha Jane Trussell on 15 Feb 1893 in Grayson County, Texas. He was born on 10 Jan 1867 in Grenada, Mississippi. He died on 01 Mar 1919 in Sherman, Texas. She married (2) WILLIAM HICKS BRAY, son of James Bray and Mary Wilson on 11 Sep 1934 in Clay County, Texas. He was born on 08 Jan 1868 in Texas. He died on 14 May 1941 in Lubbock, Texas.

More About Flora Belle Payne:
Burial: 31 Dec 1938 in West Hill Cemetery, Grayson County, Texas

Cause Of Death: Coronary Occlusion
Living In: 1920 Living with her minor children, Nina Lea and William, as a widow in Sherman, Grayson County, Texas
Living In: 1930 Living with her daughter, Nina Lea, and Nina's husband, Al Bryan, in Okemah, Okfuskee County, Oklahoma

More About Charles Edward Savage:
Burial: 03 Mar 1919 in West Hill Cemetery, Sherman, Grayson County, Texas
Cause Of Death: Heart Attack
Occupation: 1880; Farm Worker, Grayson County, Texas
Occupation: 1900 in Whitewright, Grayson County, Texas; Hardware Salesman
Occupation: 1905 in Sherman, Grayson County, Texas; Salesman
Occupation: 1910 in Sherman, Grayson County, Texas; Hardware Salesman at Hardwicke and Etter Hardware Company
Occupation: 1912 in Sherman, Grayson County, Texas; Clerk at Hardwicke and Etter Hardware Company
Occupation: 1914 in Sherman, Grayson County, Texas; Bookkeeper for Hardwicke and Etter Hardware Company
Occupation: 1916 in Sherman, Grayson County, Texas; Clerk at Hardwicke and Etter Hardware Company
Occupation: 1916 in Sherman, Grayson County, Texas; Councilman
Occupation: 1918 in Sherman, Grayson County, Texas; City Clerk

Charles Edward Savage and Flora Belle Payne had the following children:

    i. MAUDE ALEENE[8] SAVAGE was born on 27 Jul 1894 in Whitewright, Texas. She died on 29 Jan 1977 in Sherman, Texas. She married (1) JOSEPH BLEDSOE THORN, son of David Dancy Thorn and Ida Susan Bledsoe on 18 May 1916 in Sherman, Texas. He was born on 30 Dec 1892 in Eureka Springs, Arkansas. He died on 13 Nov 1976 in Whitesboro, Grayson County, Texas. She married (2) CHARLES BATSELL WINSTEAD, son of Washington Lee Winstead and May Merle Tutt on 09 Aug 1970. He was born on 25 May 1891 in Sherman, Texas. He died on 03 Aug 1973 in Albuquerque, New Mexico.

    More About Maude Aleene Savage:
    Burial: 01 Feb 1977 in West Hill Cemetery, Grayson County, Texas
    Occupation: 1940 in Sherman, Grayson County, Texas; Recreation Leader on Recreation Project

    ii. FLORA CLYDE SAVAGE was born on 26 Feb 1896 in Whitewright, Texas. She died on 15 Jan 1987 in Dallas, Texas. She married Claude Augustus Brewer, son of William Eller Brewer and Maude Elizabeth Carson on 13 Jan 1918 in Sherman, Texas. He was born on 24 Sep 1895 in Cumby, Hopkins County, Texas. He died on 30 Dec 1969 in Dallas, Texas.

    More About Flora Clyde Savage:
    Burial: Restland Memorial Park, Dallas, Dallas County, Texas
    Living In: 1920 January 19, 1920 Flora and her daughter, Bette, are living with her mother in Sherman, Grayson County, Texas.
    Occupation: 1940 in Dallas, Dallas County, Texas; Public School Teacher

Notes for Flora Clyde Savage:
Texas Death Index gives date of death as January 15, 1987.

Marriahe license was issued January 12, 1918 in Bexar County, Texas. Wedding performed by F.F. Brown, Pastor of First Baptist Church of Sherman, Texas. Date and place of wedding is not filled out on certificate. Bride's parents were Witnesses. Certificate returned to Frank R. Newton, County Clerk of Bexar County, on January 21, 1918.

-

    iii.   NINA LEA SAVAGE was born on 07 May 1900 in Whitewright, Texas. She died on 02 Jul 1982 in Edmond, Oklahoma. She married Al Bryan on 06 Nov 1921 in Sherman, Texas. He was born on 23 Jan 1899 in Texas. He died on 07 Dec 1982 in Edmond, Oklahoma.

    iv.   WILLIAM PAYNE SAVAGE was born on 23 Sep 1903 in Whitewright, Texas. He died in Jul 1970 in Oklahoma City, Oklahoma. He married Mary Bell Badgett, daughter of Claude Ray Badgett and Annie Bell Bowie on 28 Feb 1925 in Bells, Grayson County, Texas. She was born on 19 Oct 1905 in Bells, Texas. She died on 20 Feb 1964 in Houston, Texas.

More About William Payne Savage:
Burial: 22 Jul 1970 in West Hill Cemetery, Sherman, Grayson County, Texas Cause Of Death: Heart Attack
Living In: 1935 Amarillo, Texas
Living In: 1940 Living with his sister, Nina Lea and her family, in Oklahoma City, Oklahoma
Occupation: 1926 in Sherman, Grayson County, Texas; Accountant at Hardwicke and Etter Hardware Company
Occupation: 1930 in Amarillo, Texas; Bookkeeper in Wholesale Hardware
Occupation: 1932 in Amarillo, Texas; Clerk for Morrow-Thomas Hardware
Occupation: 1933 in Amarillo, Texas; Clerk for Morrow-Thomas Hardware
Occupation: 1940 in Oklahoma City, Oklahoma; Traveling Salesman for Wholesale Hardware
Military Service: U.S. Army, World War 2, (Captain)

Notes for William Payne Savage:
Found dead in his hotel room in Oklahoma City, Oklahoma. He had been dead several days so exact date of death is unknown.

More About William Hicks Bray:
Burial: 15 May 1941 in Johnson Memorial Cemetery, Munday, Knox County, Texas
Cause Of Death: Cerebral Homorhage
Occupation: 1880 in Grayson County, Texas; Works on Farm
Occupation: 1900 in Justice Precinct 6, Grayson County, Texas; Farmer
Occupation: 1910 in Chillicothe Ward 3, Hardeman County, Texas; Retail Grocery Salesman
Occupation: 1920 in Munday, Knox County, Texas; Grocery Store Salesman
Occupation: 1930 in Munday, Knox County, Texas; Merchantile Collector
Occupation: 1940 in Bowie, Montague County, Texas; Retired

29.   MARY ELIZABETH[7] PAYNE (William[6], Nathan[5], Edmund[4], Reuben[3], Thomas[2], Thomas[1]) was born on 04 Nov 1866 in Lone Oak, Texas. She died on 23 Jan 1957 in University Park, Dallas County, Texas. She married Charles W. Melson on 29 Feb 1888 in Hunt County, Texas. He was born on

06 Oct 1860 in Missouri. He died on 21 Sep 1925 in Floydada, Floyd County, Texas.

More About Mary Elizabeth Payne:
Burial: Odd Fellows Cemetery, Denton, Denton County, Texas
Living In: 1910   Living with her daughters, Mary and Addie, in Denton, Denton County, Texas
Living In: 1920   Living with her daughters, Mary and Addie, in Denton, Denton County, Texas
Living In: 1940   Living with her daughter, Addie, in Dallas, Dallas County, Texas.

More About Charles W. Melson:
Burial: 23 Sep 1925 in Whitewright, Texas
Occupation: 1900 in Whitewright, Grayson County, Texas; Manager of Bottling Company

Charles W. Melson and Mary Elizabeth Payne had the following children:

     i.   FRANK C.[8] MELSON was born in Jan 1890 in Texas.

    ii.   MARY V. MELSON was born in May 1893 in Texas.

        More About Mary V. Melson:
        Living In: 1920   Living with her mother in Denton, Denton County, Texas.
        Occupation: 1920 in Denton, Denton County, Texas; Public School Teacher

    iii.   ADDIE L. MELSON was born on 04 Feb 1897 in Texas. She died on 19 Sep 1972 in Dallas, Dallas County, Texas.

        More About Addie L. Melson:
        Burial: Odd Fellows Cemetery, Denton, Denton County, Texas
        Living In: 1920 Living with her mother in Denton, Denton County, Texas.
        Occupation: 1920 in Denton, Denton County, Texas; Public School Teacher
        Occupation: 1940 in Dallas, Dallas County, Texas; Public School English Teacher

        Notes   for   Addie   L.
        Melson: Never Married.

30.   WILLIAM EMMET[7] PAYNE (William[6], Nathan[5], Edmund[4], Reuben[3], Thomas[2], Thomas[1]) was born on 10 Feb 1872 in Texas. He died on 07 Feb 1920 in Gainsville, Texas. He married HATTIE ANN BURT. She was born on 22 Dec 1896 in Arkansas. She died on 25 Aug 1976 in Plainview, Hale County, Texas.

More About William Emmet Payne:
Living In: 1900 Living with his parents in Whitewright, Grayson County, Texas.
Living In: 1910 Township 6, Bryan County, Oklahoma
Living In: 03 Jan 1920 With his wife and sons in Kemp, Bryan County, Oklahoma.
Occupation: 1900 in Whitewright, Grayson County, Texas; Day Laborer

Notes for William Emmet Payne:
1900 Census gives July 1872 as birthdate.

More About Hattie Ann Burt:
Burial: Resthaven Cemetery, Quitaque, Briscoe County, Texas
Living In: 1930 Hattie and her four children are living with her brother, Wesley Burt, and his

family in Precinct 4, Motley County, Texas.
Occupation: 1930 in Precinct 4, Motley County, Texas; Farm Laborer

William Emmet Payne and Hattie Ann Burt had the following children:

    i. WILLIAM LEWIS[8] PAYNE was born on 11 Mar 1917 in Oklahoma. He died on 05 Jun 1933 in Kalgary,Garza County, Texas.

       More About William Lewis Payne:
       Burial: 06 Jun 1933 in Afton, Texas
       Cause Of Death: Pneumonia

    ii. JOE BAILEY PAYNE was born on 18 Jul 1919 in Oklahoma. He died on 01 Nov 2007 in Multnomah County, oregon.

       More About Joe Bailey Payne:
       Living In: 1930 Living with his mother and uncle, Wesley Burt, in Precinct 4, Motley County, Texas.
       Living In: 1940 Living with his mother and step father in Briscoe County, Texas
       Occupation: 1940 in Briscoe County, Texas; Laborer at Gravel Pit

31. **LESLIE NEWTON[7] PAYNE** (William[6], Nathan[5], Edmund[4], Reuben[3], Thomas[2], Thomas[1]) was born on 14 Jun 1874 in Texas. He died on 16 Apr 1932 in Gainesville, Cooke County, Texas. He married Lela Belle Biffle, daughter of J. T. Biffle and Mary Jane Brown on 01 May 1901 in Cooke County, Texas. She was born on 05 Oct 1882 in Myra, Cooke County, Texas. She died on 23 Dec 1948 in Myra, Cooke County, Texas.

More About Leslie Newton Payne:
Burial: 18 Apr 1932 in Reed Cemetery, Myra, Cooke County, Texas
Living In: 1900 Living with his parents in Whitewright, Grayson County, Texas.
Occupation: 1900 in Whitewright, Grayson County, Texas; Fire Insurance Agent
Occupation: 1910 in El Paso, El Paso county, Texas; Local Manager for Oil Company
Occupation: 1920 in San Antonio, Bexas County, Texas; Commercial Traveler for Tires
Occupation: 1930 in Fort Worth, Tarrant County, Texas; Salesman for Oil Supply Company

More About Lela Belle Biffle:
Burial: 24 Dec 1948 in Reed Cemetery, Myra, Cooke County, Texas

Leslie Newton Payne and Lela Belle Biffle had the following child:

    i. LELA MAE[8] PAYNE was born about 1902 in Texas.

32. **METTIE KATHRYN[7] PAYNE** (William[6], Nathan[5], Edmund[4], Reuben[3], Thomas[2], Thomas[1]) was born on 4 Dec 1877 in Texas. She died on 14 Apr 1947 in Fort Worth, Tarrant County, Texas. She married Marion Pace, son of W. A. Pace and Sarah Hawkins after 30 May 1912. He was born on 11 Jul 1852 in Indiana. He died on 17 Jul 1930 in Cleburne, Johnson County, Texas.

More About Mettie Kathryn Payne:
Burial: 16 Apr 1947 in Cleburne Memorial Cemetery, Cleburne, Johnson County, Texas
Living In: 1910 Living with her mother in Denton, Denton County, Texas.

More About Marion Pace:
Burial: 19 Jul 1930 in Cleburne Memorial Cemetery, Cleburne, Johnson County, Texas
Occupation: 1920 in Cleburne, Johnson County, Texas; Manager of his own ranch

Occupation: 1930 in Cleburne, Johnson County, Texas; Retired

Marion Pace and Mettie Kathryn Payne had the following children:

    i. MARION PAYNE[8] PACE was born on 27 Apr 1914 in Texas. She died on 09 Aug 2002. She married LON WORTH EVANS. He was born on 25 Dec 1911 in Texas. He died on 11 Dec 1992.

        More About Marion Payne Pace:
        Burial: Greenwood Memorial Park, Fort Worth, Tarrant County, Texas

    ii. FRANCES PACE was born about 1916 in Texas.

33. **FRANCES EDITH[7] PAYNE** (William[6], Nathan[5], Edmund[4], Reuben[3], Thomas[2], Thomas[1]) was born on 18 Dec 1880 in Lone Oak, Texas. She died on 04 Jan 1957 in University Park, Dallas County, Texas. She married **JOSEPH NELSON FENDER**. He was born on 02 Jan 1877 in Kaufman County, Texas. He died on 28 Nov 1967 in Dallas, Dallas County, Texas.

More About Frances Edith Payne:
Burial: College Mound Cemetery, Terrell, Kaufman County, Texas
Living In: 1910 Living with her mother in Denton, Denton County, Texas.

More About Joseph Nelson Fender:
Burial: College Mound Cemetery, Terrell, Kaufman County, Texas
Occupation: 1920 in Dallas, Dallas County, Texas; Machinery Salesman
Occupation: 1930 in Amarillo, Potter County, Texas; Commercial Traveler for Wholesale Plumbing
Occupation: 1940 in University Park, Dallas County, Texas; Salesman of Oil Well Machinery

Joseph Nelson Fender and Frances Edith Payne had the following children:

    i. JOE GRAHAM[8] FENDER was born on 12 Sep 1914 in Dallas, Dallas County, Texas. He died on 25 Nov 2007. He married MARIAN LONGNECKER. She was born on 05 Oct 1926. She died on 11 Aug 1987.

        More About Joe Graham Fender:
        Burial: College Mound Cemetery, Terrell, Kaufman County, Texas
        Living In: 1940 Living with his parents in University Park, Dallas County, Texas.

    ii. FRANCES PAYNE FENDER was born on 27 Jun 1917 in Dallas, Dallas County, Texas. She died on 04 Nov 1966 in University Park, Dallas County, Texas.

        More About Frances Payne Fender:
        Burial: College Mound Cemetery, Terrell, Kaufman County, Texas
        Living In: 1940 Living with her parents in University Park, Dallas County, Texas.

34. **FLOYD ALEXANDER[7] PAYNE** (Andrew Alexander[6], Nathan[5], Edmund[4], Reuben[3], Thomas[2], Thomas[1]) was born on 15 May 1888 in Lone Oak, Hunt County, Texas. He died on 16 Sep 1966 in San Angelo, Texas. He married **WILLIE WALSH**. She was born in 1892 in Texas.

Floyd Alexander Payne and Willie Walsh had the following children:

    i. J. D.[8] PAYNE was born in 1909 in Lone Oak, Hunt County, Texas.

    ii. OLETA FERN PAYNE was born on 28 Jul 1913 in Lone Oak, Hunt County, Texas. She died on 03 Oct 1989 in Crowley, Texas. She married ROY EDSON ADAMS.

35.   **BERYL**[7] **SCOTT** (Amelia Mildred[6] Payne, Nathan[5] Payne, Edmund[4] Payne, Reuben[3] Payne, Thomas[2] Payne, Thomas[1] Payne) was born on 08 Mar 1889 in Lone Oak, Hunt County, Texas. She died on 24 Jun 1965 in Fort Worth, Tarrant County, Texas. She married **J. H. WRIGHT**. He was born about 1885 in Missouri.

More About Beryl Scott:
Burial: 25 Jun 1965 in Greenwood Memorial Park, Fort Worth, Tarrant County, Texas
Occupation: 1930 in Fort Worth, Tarrant County, Texas; Cosmetologist in Beauty Parlor

More About J. H. Wright:
Occupation: 1910 in Fort Worth, Tarrant County, Texas; General Repair Laborer

J. H. Wright and Beryl Scott had the following child:

    i.   OPAL[8] WRIGHT was born about 1917 in Texas.

        More About Opal Wright:
        Occupation: 1930 in Fort Worth, Tarrant County, Texas; Insurance Stenographer

36.   **ANICE LOU**[7] **PAYNE** (Henry[6], Nathan[5], Edmund[4], Reuben[3], Thomas[2], Thomas[1]) was born on 24 May 1884 in Lone Oak, Texas. She died on 03 Jul 1978 in Andrews, Texas. She married George Edmond Moxley about 1903. He was born in Mar 1884 in Texas. He died on 06 Jan 1965.

More About Anice Lou Payne:
Burial: Andrews Cemetery, Andrews, Texas

More About George Edmond Moxley: Burial:
Andrews Cemetery, Andrews, Texas

George Edmond Moxley and Anice Lou Payne had the following children:

    i.   GEORGE HENRY[8] MOXLEY. He died on 06 Jan 1965 in Andrews, Texas.

    ii.   LOYLE ANICE MOXLEY was born on 11 Jul 1904 in Lone Oak, Texas. She died on 31 Jan 1982 in Andrews, Texas. She married LEWIS CARTER DOWNING. He was born on 19 Nov 1897. He died on 21 Aug 1984 in Andrews, Texas.

    iii.   MARY MOXLEY was born in 1906. She died in 1937. She married ALFRED BYNUM.

    iv.   JOSEPH MOXLEY was born on 27 Feb 1910 in Lone Oak, Texas. He died on 08 Aug 1910 in Lone Oak, Texas.

    v.   BOYD MOXLEY was born on 16 Aug 1911. He died on 12 Jan 2001 in Andrews, Texas. He married OLA MAY MORSE.

    vi.   RAYBURN MOXLEY was born on 13 Apr 1913 in Lone Oak, Texas. He died on 22 May 1977 in Andrews, Texas. He married FLO HELEN FORBUS. She was born on 04 Aug 1912 in Abilene, Texas. She died on 30 Jul 1997 in Cedar Park, Texas.

    vii.   WILLIAM BENTON MOXLEY was born on 25 Feb 1915. He died on 07 Sep 2000 in Andrews, Texas. He married SALLIE MARY FORT.

    viii.   ELVA ARLENE MOXLEY was born on 07 Jun 1917 in Lone Oak, Texas. She married

Jeff Lonis.

     ix.   J. W. Moxley was born in 1919. He married Winona (unknown).

37.   John Crenshaw[7] Payne (Henry[6], Nathan[5], Edmund[4], Reuben[3], Thomas[2], Thomas[1]) was born on 6 Dec 1885 in Lone Oak, Texas. He died on 16 Mar 1958 in Spur, Texas. He married Bessie L. Ensey in 1911. She was born in 1895 in Texas.

More About John Crenshaw Payne:
Living In: 1910 Living with his mother in Justice Precinct 8, Hunt County, Texas.
Occupation: 1910 in Justice Precinct 8, Hunt County, Texas; Farmer

John Crenshaw Payne and Bessie L. Ensey had the following children:
     i. John Jackson[8] Payne was born on 11 Aug 1913. He died on 10 Sep 1985 in Fort Worth, Texas. He married Cleo Barker. He married Imogene Hall.

     ii.   Alfred Payne was born in 1916. He married Omer Inez Beason.

38.   Nathan Alexander[7] Payne (Henry[6], Nathan[5], Edmund[4], Reuben[3], Thomas[2], Thomas[1]) was born on 31 May 1887 in Lone Oak, Texas. He died on 09 Aug 1953 in Lubbock, Texas. He married Lillie Mae Jenkins, daughter of Horace Jenkins and Mary Fortenberry on 10 Nov 1907 in Lone Oak, Texas. She was born on 16 Jul 1891 in Lone Oak, Texas. She died on 17 Mar 1963 in Lubbock, Texas.

More About Nathan Alexander Payne:
Burial: 11 Aug 1953 in Tech Memorial Park, Lubbock,
Texas
Cause Of Death: Cerebral Vascular Accident
Occupation: Farmer

More About Lillie Mae Jenkins:
Burial: Resthaven Cemetery, Lubbock, Texas

Nathan Alexander Payne and Lillie Mae Jenkins had the following children:
     i.   Ameral[8] Payne was born on 06 Oct 1908 in Lone Oak, Texas. He died on 10 Apr 1981 in Lubbock, Texas. He married Ruby Cristine Kennedy, daughter of L. F. Kennedy and Iva McWhorter on 30 Jun 1932 in Lamesa, Texas. She was born on 08 May 1910 in Lamesa, Texas. She died on 27 Feb 1987 in Lubbock, Texas.

     More About Ameral Payne:
     Burial: Resthaven Cemetery, Lubbock, Texas

     ii.   Mary Frances Payne was born on 11 Jul 1929 in Lubbock, Texas. She died on 01 Aug 1972 in Lubbock, Texas. She married Harold Franklin Wall on 06 Feb 1949.

     More About Mary Frances Payne:
     Burial: Resthaven Cemetery, Lubbock, Texas

39.   Catherine Zelma[7] Payne (Henry[6], Nathan[5], Edmund[4], Reuben[3], Thomas[2], Thomas[1]) was born on 16 Feb 1894 in Lone Oak, Texas. She died in Dec 1982. She married Jim Bailey in 1912. He died in 1952.

More About Catherine Zelma Payne:
Burial: Resthaven Cemetery, Lubbock, Texas

Jim Bailey and Catherine Zelma Payne had the following children:

    i.   ELEANOR[8] BAILEY was born in 1915. She married J. WELDON BENNET. He was born on 28 Aug 1919. He died on 28 Jun 1996.

    ii.   KATHRYN BAILEY was born on 08 Dec 1919. She died on 03 Jun 1994. She married Eddy Czerwiec about 1940. He was born on 07 Aug 1920. He died in Aug 1944.

        More About Kathryn Bailey:
        Burial: Resthaven Cemetery, Lubbock, Texas

40.   **HENRY YOAKUM[7] PAYNE** (Henry[6], Nathan[5], Edmund[4], Reuben[3], Thomas[2], Thomas[1]) was born on 8 Jan 1896 in Lone Oak, Texas. He died on 28 Jun 1921 in Lubbock, Texas. He married Myrtle Ensley on 25 Oct 1917. She was born about 1900 in Texas.

More About Henry Yoakum Payne:
Burial: Lone Oak Cemetery, Hunt County, Texas

Henry Yoakum Payne and Myrtle Ensley had the following children:

    i.   MAYOMA MAXINE[8] PAYNE was born in 1917 in Hunt County, Texas. She died on 22 Nov 1917 in Hunt County, Texas.

        More About Mayoma Maxine Payne:
        Burial: Lone Oak Cemetery, Hunt County, Texas

    ii.   HELEN PAYNE was born on 23 Oct 1918. She died on 15 Dec 1987 in Mineral Wells, Texas. She married MARCUS J. LEE. He was born on 17 Jun 1913. He died on 15 Dec 1987 in Mineral Wells, Texas. She married POPE KEARLEY.

41.   **ARLON GODBY[7] PAYNE** (Henry[6], Nathan[5], Edmund[4], Reuben[3], Thomas[2], Thomas[1]) was born on 03 Apr 1900 in Lone Oak, Texas. He died on 26 Aug 1961 in Harrison, Arkansas. He married **NONA MAE ARMSTRONG**. She was born on 11 Mar 1899. She died on 28 Oct 1979 in Arkansas.

More About Arlon Godby Payne:
Burial: City of Lubbock Cemetery, Lubbock, Texas
Living In: 1920 Living with his brother, Lewis, in Justice Precinct 8, Hunt County, Texas.
Occupation: 1920 in Justice Precinct 8, Hunt County, Texas; Farm Laborer

More About Nona Mae Armstrong:
Burial: City of Lubbock Cemetery, Lubbock, Texas

Arlon Godby Payne and Nona Mae Armstrong had the following child:

    i.   DOROTHY SUE[8] PAYNE was born on 31 Aug 1924. She died on 16 Jul 1989 in Green Forest, Arkansas. She married HARVEY MARCUS PICKETT.

        More About Dorothy Sue Payne:
        Burial: Alpena, Arkansas

42. **FANNIE SUE**[7] **WILLIAMS** (Mary Katherine[6] Payne, Nathan[5] Payne, Edmund[4] Payne, Reuben[3] Payne, Thomas[2] Payne, Thomas[1] Payne) was born on 30 Apr 1883 in Lone Oak, Hunt County, Texas. She died on 24 Jun 1956 in Greenville, Texas. She married Albert L. Dodd on 29 Nov 1902 in Hunt County, Texas. He was born on 02 Nov 1879 in Texas. He died on 07 Apr 1961 in Austin, Texas.

Notes for Fannie Sue Williams:
Fannie and Joseph are apparently twins born six days apart.

More About Albert L. Dodd:
Burial: 08 Apr 1961 in Lone Oak Cemetery, Lone Oak, Texas

Albert L. Dodd and Fannie Sue Williams had the following child:

      i.   ABBEY MAXWELL[8] DODD was born on 11 Mar 1907 in Texas. He died on 17 Sep 1996 in Los Angeles, California. He married Virginia Lee Hobday on 25 Dec 1934 in Yuma, Arizona. She was born on 30 May 1918 in California. She died on 01 Jul 1982 in Los Angeles, California.

43. **NATHAN ORAL**[7] **PAYNE** (Nathan[6], Nathan[5], Edmund[4], Reuben[3], Thomas[2], Thomas[1]) was born on 8 Mar 1896 in Lone Oak, Hunt County, Texas. He died on 28 Jul 1969 in Burnsville community, Sebastion County, Arkansas. He married **NELLIE OWEN**. She was born on 11 Sep 1898 in Texas. She died on 13 Feb 1976 in Fort Smith, Arkansas.

More About Nathan Oral Payne:
Burial: 30 Jul 1969 in Liberty Cemetery, Greenwood, Sebastian County, Arkansas

Notes for Nathan Oral Payne:
Greenwood Democrat Thursday July 31, 1969:

Funeral service for Nathan O. Payne, 73 was held Wednesday at 2 p.m. at McConnell Funeral Chapel in Greenwood with Rev. Dan Evans and Rev. Elmus C. Brown officiating. Burial was in Liberty Cemetery.
Mr. Payne died Monday at his home in the Burnsville Community. He was a retired railroad man. Survivors include his wife, Nellie; one daughter, Mrs. Edward Thomas, Greenwood; one brother Grady, Fort Worth, Tex; and two sisters, Mrs Pearl Shepard and Mrs. Grace Aldrich, both of Ft. Worth.
Pallbearers were Carol Cesar, Bud Jones, Bill Johnson, Means Wilkinson, Willie Lewis and Gene Winford.

More About Nellie Owen:
Burial: 16 Feb 1976 in Liberty Cemetery, Greenwood, Sebastian County, Arkansas

Notes for Nellie Owen:
Greenwood Democrat Thursday 19 Feb 1976, Page 9:

Funeral services for Mrs. Nellie Payne, 77, of Greenwood, who died Friday in a Fort Smith hospital, were held at 2 p.m. Monday in McConnell Memorial Chapel. Burial was in Liberty Cemetery. Survivors include a daughter, Mrs. Ed Thomas of Greenwood and a sister, Mrs. Luvena Farmer of Boulder, Colo.
Funeral Home Record: Father is David Franklin Owen

Nathan Oral Payne and Nellie Owen had the following child:

  i. MATTIE LEE[8] PAYNE was born on 25 Mar 1918 in Fort Worth, Tarrant County, Texas.

www.ingramcontent.com/pod-product-compliance
Lightning Source LLC
Chambersburg PA
CBHW080818280726
48660CB00018B/3506